DRINK

PINK

DRINK
PINK

A CELEBRATION OF
ROSÉ

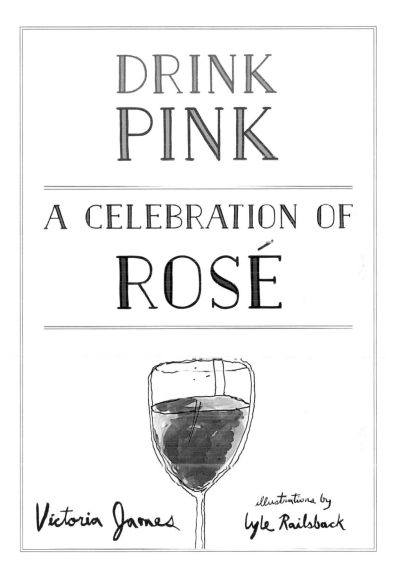

Victoria James

illustrations by
Lyle Railsback

HARPER
DESIGN

An Imprint of HarperCollins Publishers

DEDICATED TO

LAURA JAMES

CONTENTS

Rosé is probably the most unpretentious and democratic of all wines. Something you drink while playing boules or when going mushrooming—a true vin de copain.

JACQUES PÉPIN
RENOWNED FRENCH CHEF

INTRODUCTION

I HAD MY FIRST TASTE OF WINE WHEN I WAS NINE YEARS OLD. WHEN MY Grandma Willie wasn't looking, I snuck a swig from her glass. She was a big fan of sitting on the porch at night, reading romance novels, and sipping White Zinfandel. Cooled down with a cup full of ice, the pink drink seemed like such a pleasant escape.

Years later at twenty-one, I would take my first legal sip of rosé. I was feverishly studying for my sommelier exam and tasting up to one hundred wines a day. *Taste. Swoosh. Think. Spit.* Every day I would go through the painstaking process of trying wines from around the world to register their characteristics. Although barely legal, I passed my exam and became the youngest sommelier in the country.

A few years passed. My obsession with exams dwindled as I traveled to some of the most beautiful places in the world, like France, Portugal, Chile, Italy, California, and Switzerland. I worked in vineyards alongside winemakers learning about the heart and soul of wine. Long lunches flowed into dinners filled with laughter and stories. I fell in love with centuries of tradition and the humble farmers who dedicated themselves to their land, and still do.

Wine is one of the most competitive industries in the world. It is a constant battle to stay relevant. Every day I tackle a bit more of the never-ending world of wine, making sure my knowledge is always up to date. I think these pressures eventually wear down a lot of sommeliers.

However, I have a trick: *Drink more rosé.* For me, no other wine embodies the *joie de vivre* like rosé. There is nothing daunting about pink wine. It does not force you to recall complicated French classifications put in place during the 1800s or rules governing vineyard management.

After a few sips of rosé, I am reminded that *this* is what wine is all about, pleasure and simplicity. Although my palate has evolved past White Zinfandel, I still hold onto my childhood delight in pink wine.

ROSÉ IS
OLD SCHOOL

*The history of the pink drink goes back a
lot further than you might think. From
Ancient Greece to California, it has
always been a part of wine culture.*

THE GREEKS AND THE ROMANS—
THE BIRTH OF ROSÉ
(EIGHTH CENTURY BCE—MID 100s BCE)

Amphictyon, a Greek God that some traditions note as having been born from the earth, created pale wines of rosé color by simply mixing red wine with water. This less potent beverage helped minimize quarreling during meetings of his councilors who often leaned too heavily on wine for confidence.

In ancient Greece, white and red grapes were harvested together and pressed quickly to allow fermentation to begin. The impatience for drinkable wine usually outweighed the desire to explore higher quality winemaking. As a result, almost all wine was a natural light pink color.

Eventually, the Greeks and Romans explored separating grapes by color. They also allowed the skins to macerate with the juice for pigment, eventually creating red wines. However, these early examples were often tannic and hard to drink. For quite some time, the general preference leaned toward the less harsh, lighter-colored wines. Rosé remained the beverage of choice for centuries.

THE FIRST WINES IN FRANCE WERE ROSÉ.
(SIXTH CENTURY BCE—EARLY NINETEENTH CENTURY)

In the sixth century BCE, people known as the Phocaeans, from an ancient Ionian Greek city, set sail. From Greece, they brought grape vines to Massalia (modern day Marseille) in southern France. The wines they made there were naturally light pink in color. Why? Well, pigment in wine comes from the grape skin. (Next time you are eating a grape, bite it in half and look at the inside. You will notice the pulp and juice are clear.) By not letting the skins of the grapes sit with the juice, the finished product only picks up a bit of color. These rosés would forever have a home in the South of France.

In the second century BCE, the Romans landed in Provence. They had already heard all about the "pink wines of Massalia." They took these coveted wines and used their super-connected trade networks to make them popular around the Mediterranean.

In the Middle Ages, it was rumored that Bordeaux created violet-colored rosé. The wine picked up a nickname known as "Clareit" (in Latin, *claritas* means clarity). These gently colored wines soon became fashionable around France.

In the twelfth century, Bordeaux came under British rule. The English loved their newfound pink wine dearly. Writer Samuel Johnson famously stated, "He who aspires to be a serious wine drinker must drink Claret." Until the late 1900s, the English and their precious "Claret" were inseparable.

In the nineteenth century, French tourists started to flock to places like the Côte d'Azur in southern France. After a long day of playing pétanque and swimming in

the sea, they would relax with a chilled glass of rosé. All of a sudden, these local wines became a symbol of glamour, leisure, and summer.

For many, rosé also became a simple *vin de soif* (wine to quench thirst), something to drink while you were cooking or to serve as an apéritif before dinner. It was not a fussy wine. Many parents would even serve it to their children as a treat.

Jacques Pépin told me that he first drank rosé when he was only six or seven years old. "It was wonderful. My father would start putting a tablespoon of rosé in a glass of water, just to change the color a little bit and get a taste of what it is. You have to understand, back then, there was no soda or anything. There was water and then there was wine, that was it."

PORTUGAL: MATEUS AND LANCERS
(1940s–1970s)

If you have never heard of Mateus and Lancers, you might be surprised to know that these products are what many blame for ruining rosé's reputation. Let's take a look at both of them a bit more.

Fernando van Zeller Guedes said he created the infamous Mateus rosé because of bed bugs. While traveling around the Douro in Portugal in the 1940s, Guedes rarely slept due to bed bug infestations at the local hotels. As a result, he would stay up at night, constantly thinking and reviewing his notes on wine. Apparently, on one of these sleepless nights, he came up with the idea of a wine that would appeal to both "women and younger generations." He also decided to create a bottle shaped like a soldier's canteen. Some viewed this as fuel for the war on "serious" wine.

This sweet and pétillant (slightly sparkling) wine hit the market in late 1943. It was an overnight success. Mateus became rich and everyone else grew up thinking rosé was nothing more than cheap, poorly made juice.

Around the same time Mateus came onto the market, an American wine merchant named Henry Behar sailed to Portugal to visit the Port estate, Maria da Fonseca. Port is a fortified wine, dark in color, full in body, and loaded with sugar.

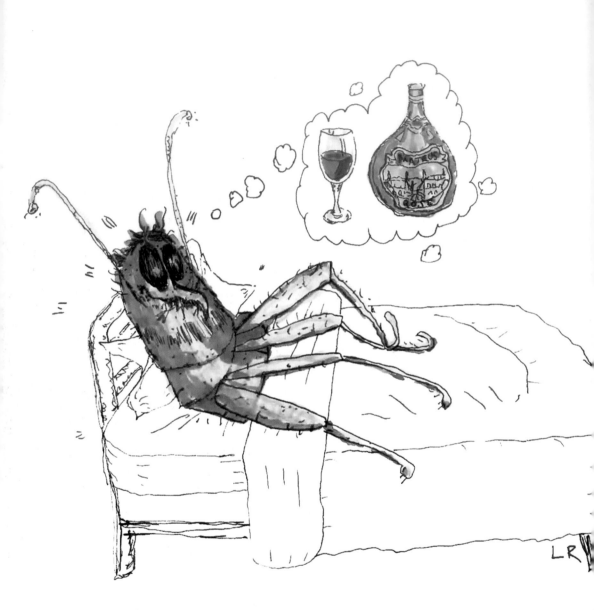

While there, Behar tasted a wine named "Faisca," which was slightly sweet and pink in color. He found the wine quite refreshing. At the time, it probably was. He had spent all day tasting Ports! Maria da Fonseca struck a deal with Behar, and he brought Faisca back to the United States, distributing the brand that would soon become an icon.

Since the name Faisca was considered to be too close to *fiasco*, for the American market, Behar instead named it after his favorite Velasquez painting, "Las Lanzas." The bottle shape and material were also what set it apart from other wines on store shelves. It was a squat ceramic bottle. Americans couldn't resist it. Before too long, disaster struck, though. There is a reason that wine, especially a youthful rosé, is bottled in glass: to protect it from oxygen. In ceramic, the wine quickly oxidized (turned brown and gross). Not good for something that was supposed to be easy-drinking and versatile.

Eventually the bottle changed to thick glass and then to frosted glass. To this day, Lancers is still quite popular in Central Europe simply because most people think it is liquor instead of wine. It is also very cheap and very sweet, which some people like.

Slowly, people started to turn their noses up at the quality of Mateus. Sales dropped. In an effort to revive the brand, compelling advertising campaigns featuring everyone from Jimi Hendrix to the Queen of England ran all over the United Kingdom and leaked out to the rest of the world. The wine was instantly back in fashion. After the Carnation Revolution in 1974, when democracy returned to Portugal, the United States rushed to import twenty million cases of Mateus in the hope of continuing their established relationship with the brand. Americans were not keen to lose their pink fix.

Kermit Lynch, of Kermit Lynch Wine Merchant, started his now-famous business in the 1970s, in a small shop in Berkeley, California. He says,

> When I opened my business, and when I grew up in wine, rosé had a terrible reputation. In the serious wine community, people did not drink rosé, it wasn't considered real wine, it was just something made from the rotten grapes that could not go into the red. That was the attitude of the serious wine community. There were a few rosés, back then, one of them in a weird jug, they were just wretched! When I started, I didn't have any rosé for sale, of course I had a teensy store, I wasn't attracting the Lancers crowd. I had people come in and ask for Meursault and Echezeaux, things like that.

Mateus and Lancers changed the way people think of rosé. These novelty items made the public think all pink wine was inexpensive, sweet, and made in bulk. Many recall times fondly referred to as "Lancers poisoning" or the "Mateus hangover."

A few coming-of-age stories worldwide would not be complete without the beverage. It is the "Two Buck Chuck" of the world. Very few of us are fortunate enough to start our drinking careers in Bordeaux or Burgundy. More often than not, teenagers will scrape together whatever loose change they can find and send their oldest looking friend into the wine shop to buy a bottle. More often than not, youthful palates love wine that tastes more like juice (their beverage of choice in the not-so-distant past).

So thank you, Mateus and Lancers, for giving our parents, grandparents, and their friends a cheap way to get tipsy. We are glad you didn't tarnish our palates forever, although you sure came close.

HOW AMERICA LEARNED TO LOVE ROSÉ
(1869–1990s)

Rosé is kind of fashionable now in the United States. It wasn't forty or thirty years ago, but I would always have rosé around.
—JACQUES PÉPIN

George West of El Pinal Winery in Lodi, California, made what is documented as the first White Zinfandel in 1869. The viticultural commissioner at the time found the wine impressive and began to advocate Zinfandel's use outside of red wine. For over a century, this pink wine gained little traction.

It's the 1970s in California, and a winery called Sutter Home is famous for its dark and intense Amador County Zinfandel. One day, the winemaker, Bob Trinchero, decides he wants to make this wine even more concentrated and inkier. But how does he do that with just grapes? He comes up with the idea of pressing the grapes as he normally would, but capturing the first bit of juice that comes out and separating it. This "free run juice" is light in color, since it hasn't had a lot of contact with the grape skins. Now the remaining grapes are ready to be pressed and make a wine of extreme intensity. Without that watery pink juice lightening up the batch, his Zinfandel became much more powerful.

So what did he do with this light-pink free-run juice? Sure, he could have thrown it away, but Trinchero, ever the admirer of French rosés, fermented and barrel-aged the liquid. Since there was so little of it, there was no point in shipping it off to customers. Instead, it was relegated to the winery tasting room for the first year.

I wasn't alive at that time, so I am not sure what the wine tasted like, but it was probably the most "French-style" (i.e., mineral-driven, dry, low alcohol) rosé Sutter Home ever produced. Trinchero even gave his first experiment the nickname of *Oeil de Perdrix* which in French translates to "eye of the partridge." This term dates back to the Middle Ages in the Champagne region of France. Wines with a pink color were called this as a reference to the pale pink color of the eye of a partridge struggling in death's grip. Such a grave name for a marvelous wine!

The United States government wasn't having Trinchero's pet name, and they insisted that a description of the wine be printed in English on the label. As a result, in very small print, "a white zinfandel wine" was included on the bottle.

In 1975, everything changed. The story the winery tells is that a "stuck fermentation" occurred. In essence, the sugar could not fully convert to alcohol. As a result, the wine produced was slightly sweet. Instead of trying to fix the problem or relegate the product to the tasting room only, they decided to take their chances. They opened the floodgates and released (slightly sweet) Sutter Home White Zinfandel. Americans absolutely loved it. After all, this idea came from how the beloved Mateus and Lancers were made. Now, though, White Zinfandel could support local farmers.

White Zinfandel spread like wildfire. In the 1980s, it was one of America's most popular wine brands. Eventually, people like my Grandmother Willie were buying bottles in bulk. In the 1990s, the world of rosé and the world of fine wine were completely separate. Sommeliers would never serve a bottle of White Zinfandel because serious wine drinkers would never ask for it. Rajat Parr, previously the Wine Director for Michael Mina restaurants, was a sommelier at that time in San Francisco.

> No one cared about it, no one thought about it, no one drank it. At the time, there wasn't rosé made for the purpose of being rosé. A winemaker maybe had some leftover grapes or something that didn't ripen and that was what the rosé was. No one was going out and saying, "I am going to make great rosé."

Relegated to cafés and cheap restaurants, the wine lay dormant for almost fifteen years. "From 1996 to 2009 I didn't serve a single rosé. Never ever. It wasn't until we opened RN74 in San Francisco that we started to serve rosé," Parr adds. Now, he is the winemaker/partner at Domaine de la Côte and Sandhi in Santa Barbara. At Sandhi, they have made high-quality and delicious still and sparkling Pinot Noir rosés. Something Parr would never have been able to do twenty years ago.

ROSÉ TODAY AND TOMORROW

Not too long ago, a guest at the restaurant where I work as the sommelier was fervently flipping through the pages of the wine list. When I offered to assist him, he sighed in relief. A very thick French accent accompanied his words, "Last year I had the most amazing rosé here. I could not find it anywhere in Europe. It is from Clear Lake. Do you still have it?" He was referring to an Arnot Roberts Touriga Nacional Rosé from California that we luckily had a bottle or two of left. I couldn't believe this gentleman was so excited to taste an American rosé again. But then, again, why not? It was delicious.

Some argue that the rosé craze in the United States is just a phase. But many experts disagree. They see this not as a trend but rather as the introduction of a new style. Kermit Lynch, one of the top importers of French and Italian wine in the United States, adds, "I think now rosé has its place, just like white and red and sparkling." Americans are slowly learning more about wine and gaining a deeper appreciation. Rosé is simply a result of this education.

In the early 2000s, rosé's popularity started to build. Resorts and beach destinations around the United States started stocking pink French wine. The Franco-fascination grew, and many places like André Balazs' Sunset Beach property on Shelter Island in New York starting sporting pétanque courts. Keen on living the authentic southern French lifestyle, rosé starting flowing endlessly. Celebrities like Drew Barrymore and Angelina Jolie along with Brad Pitt started making rosé.

Rosé was suddenly mainstream. Social media turned the pink beverage into a superstar. Instagram stars like Josh Ostrovsky ("The Fat Jew") claimed, "Rosé is like puppies, if you hate it you are an absolute monster." He went on to collaborate on a product called "White Girl Rosé," a California Sauvignon Blanc and Zinfandel blend. Hundreds of thousands of bottles have been sold.

In France, clever collaborations also have taken place. Jeremy Seysses of the highly acclaimed Domaine Dujac and Aubert de Villaine of the outstanding Domaine de la Romanée-Conti, where some of the most expensive wines in the world are made, co-founded Domaine Triennes. Located in the Var, not too far from the Jolie-Pitt owned Château Miraval, Seysses and de Villaine started producing tasty rosés.

Sommeliers from all over the United States rushed to include the wine on their lists. In the summer of 2014, almost every restaurant I went to was pouring it by the glass.

Like the baguette or the beret, we have adopted rosé into American culture. The charming nature of the beverage is hard to deny. As domestic and international examples have drastically improved in quality, it is no longer considered a guilty pleasure. Men have looked past the pink coloring and embraced "brosé" remarks. Rosé is exactly what the wine world needed, a unpretentious but delicious option.

So is the rosé trend fleeting or forever? Sommelier Rajat Parr assures us, "Oh no, rosé, it's here to stay."

PRODUCING
PINK JUICE

How is rosé made exactly?
To achieve a specific style,
careful decisions must be made by the
winemaker. Although some argue
certain methods are better than others,
each has its own merits.

HOW ROSÉ IS MADE

Crafting a delicious rosé is no mere accident. Although it might be fun to think of
the creation of rosé as a magical process, the
methods for making this enchanting wine
are actually straightforward.

Today, wine drinkers are demanding
high-quality rosé. As a result, winemakers are putting a lot of thought into how to
make exceptional pink wines. They are pay-
ing attention to vineyard sites, yields, wine-
making techniques, and vineyard management. But all that complicated stuff aside,
how exactly do you make rosé, anyway? There are essentially three main ways you
can go about it.

1. SAIGNÉE

In French, *saignée* translates to "bleeding,"
which is exactly what our little grape friends
do. The first juice that runs off from pressing
red grapes is isolated. This light-red wine is separated from the darker juice and it is reborn as
rosé. Many will argue that this is the best way
to make rosé. Since the process is extremely
gentle, the resulting wines tend toward softness
and elegance.

In this process, the rosé is not the ultimate goal but rather a by-product. The
darker colored juice after saigneé will be turned into red wine. Back in the day, a lot
of winemakers, like Bob Trinchero from Sutter Home Winery, used this method to
concentrate their red wines. In the saignée method, only a little bit of wine is bled
off and therefore only a bit of rosé is made.

Perhaps the reason saignée rosés are prized is due to supply and demand. Since less is made, the scarcity alone drives up the value. Or perhaps it's because they are delicious. Either way, keep in mind that other methods hold merit, too, and are more common.

2. SKIN CONTACT

Some top-notch winemakers will treat their red grapes like they are white. That is, they will pick them and press them right away. The skins, therefore, don't have a lot of time to add color to the juice. The resulting wine is a very light shade of pink. If a darker and more pow erful style of rosé is desired, the wine- maker can choose to macerate the skins

with the juice before pressing. This is a tricky game to play. Although the juice will pick up more color and aromatics as it sits with the skins (this is how red wine is made), it will also pick up some tannin and bitterness. The latter two characteristics are usually found undesirable in rosé. Therefore, the producer must be careful in monitoring the maceration process. The skin contact method is sensitive, but can create a wide range of styles, from structured and powerful rosés to fine and delicate ones. The versatility of this method tends to make it the most popular.

3. BLENDING

This method is one of extremes. It is used for low-quality wine but also for some of the best and most expensive rosés on the market. Essentially you take some white wine and mix it with red wine. Voilà! Pink wine. This is considered an unfavor- able means of production in most places, though. The resulting wines are usually bland and of low quality. In fact, in France, this method is illegal. If you do this, you cannot call it rosé there. There is one exception in France, however: the region of Champagne. Here, blending is considered an art form since Champagne belongs to an elusive category of wines.

Elsewhere in France, winegrowers are called *vignerons*. This translates to "a person who cultivates grapes for winemaking." Vignerons will argue that the wine is made in the vineyard. The better your *terroir* (region, climate, soil, etc.), the better the wine. When the grapes get to the winery, they do their best to not mess up what Mother Nature created. This is very different from the New World notion of winemakers.

In Champagne, however, the vigneron is more of a winemaker. They craft a style that has been a part of the culture there for centuries. To achieve the desired flavor profile, extensive measures are taken. One of the ways Champagne is manipulated is when it's used to create rosés. This process tends to be more labor intensive and requires much more skillful blending. The *chef de cave,* the person who tastes and makes the blend, must use their expertise in crafting a wine from different vineyards as well as vintages.

The whole process is mind-boggling. Hundreds of vineyard sites are separated and made into different wines. These are tasted individually and then skillfully blended together in varying proportions. In addition, wines from many vintages are added. In a non-vintage Champagne, up to twenty different years can be represented. This is how they maintain a signature "house style." So every time you pick up a NV (non-vintage) bottle of Champagne from a certain producer, it will taste the same. This is a difficult thing to achieve since every year and vineyard plot yields different results.

Usually in this blending process, still red wine is added to the final blend in order to achieve a rosé. This final addition in the recipe adds more red-fruit aromatics and makes the bubbly drink a bit more vinous. These rosés defy the whole category of pink wine. They have traditionally been some of the most expensive wines you can buy and some of the most sought-after by collectors. This is the one place in which blending can produce a high-quality rosé.

DOES ROSÉ AGE?

"Probably, but so what?" Bruce Neyers responded when I recently asked him this question. As the National Sales Manager for Kermit Lynch Wine Merchant, he sells some of the best rosés on the market. Kermit Lynch was one of the first to export high-quality European rosés to the American market. Some feel as if aging rosé is not what is important—its youthful freshness can be the key to its charm.

Others, like Rajat Parr, one of the most respected sommeliers in the industry, will argue that many rosés *can* improve with age. Wines from Bandol in France, like Domaine Tempier, are especially prized when re-visited after a few years.

Parr notes that denser wines like Bruno Clair's Marsannay rosé made from Pinot Noir in northen Burgundy get better after four or five years. "Corsican rosé, too, I bet some of the serious ones with a few years of bottle age could be really interesting."

Kermit Lynch himself added.

I have had forty-year-old Domaine Tempier rosé that was lovely, nothing like the new vintage, but still alive and a great pleasure. Also, this past year I had a 1947 rosé from Bourgueil in the Loire. It was still alive, and just fabulous and beautiful. It was Domaine Lamé Delisle Boucard. I don't import them but I did way back when. I paid them a visit and the son pulled out two 1947 reds and the rosé. I liked the rosés better than the reds, the quality of the aroma, which of course completely blew my mind. Who could imagine that could be? Well, I couldn't imagine but that's the way it was.

As the category of rosé starts to become more familiar to drinkers, questions like ageability start to arise.

Does it age? Does it matter? Should we be stocking our wine cellars with rosé? Who can resist the temptation of drinking a bottle of rosé chilling in their refrigerator, anyway?

Let the debate continue.

PINK WINE PRODUCTION

In August of 2014, panic struck: The Hamptons had run out of rosé. The shortage showed us for the first time something we might not have realized before: Americans love rosé.

As our fascination with the pink beverage grows, so does production. Winemakers are rushing to meet demands. The smart winery focuses on producing the best possible rosé they can make, in the hope of winning over consumers and gaining traction in the market.

Sadly, many wineries don't think long term. Instead, they are pumping out cheap blush wines and hoping that the consumer will chill it down so cold that they can't taste its flaws. Rajat Parr notes that "as people start to make serious rosé, the category will grow. For now, there is a lot of interest in doing so. But there is not enough to quench everyone's thirst so many producers rush to bottle and sell. There's always a push and pull."

Jeremy Seysses, winemaker of the acclaimed Domaine Dujac in Burgundy and Domaine de Triennes in Provence has expressed his worries to me.

> We are seeing a massive increase in bulk pricing. While this is a boon to the growers, this means that a number of clients are now turning to other areas for their supply, not all of them with grape varieties or climates suited to rosé. In France, we are seeing a new wave of very mediocre rosé hit the shelves and I am concerned that this will kill enthusiasm for the category.

But all hope is not lost. Many winemakers are kicking it old school and returning to the roots of rosé winemaking. Kermit Lynch loves to talk about this throwback mindset. "I think the best methods for producing rosé are the ones that some winemakers are going back to. We are going through a period, not just for rosé, but for all wines, a period of enologically correct, technologically correct wines.

Winemakers are finding out that that's not really making wines with as much interest as the old way of making wine."

Lynch goes on to add, "I really think, to my own palate, modern rosés don't remind me of wine. They smell technological to me. In the old style, the rosé smells like wine, it tastes vinous. Today, when they're done with all this blockage, sulfur, and industrial yeasts, they no longer smell like wine. They're more like a cocktail or concoction."

According to the Rosé Wine Economic Observatory between 2002 and 2013, rosé production in France increased by 31 percent. Drinkers were not far behind. In France, consumption has nearly tripled since 1990. In 2013, America was second in the world, just after France, in consumption of the pink drink.

It is sad to think that the romance of rosé has been lost, in a way. In a rush to meet demands, winemakers are creating these sterile examples that all taste the same. They have no soul, no sense of place, and are not a reflection of the centuries of tradition that made the wine what it once was.

How do we beat this influx of soulless rosé? By demanding the good stuff. Let that pink bathwater stay in the tub. Look for high-quality producers and celebrate how amazing rosé can be.

COLOR BLIND

I'm not sure how many people, if blindfolded and served
a white and rosé, could tell the difference.
I will bet you anything that most people wouldn't be able to.

KERMIT LYNCH

When asked what I would pair with a certain dish, I often recommend rosé. My guests' reactions vary. Sometimes they will take a sharp breath in and gently mention they prefer red, or they'll scoff and dismiss the category altogether. But when they give the wine a chance, they are often pleasantly surprised.

In 2002, Calvin Trillin wrote an article for *The New Yorker,* "The Red and the White." He spoke about a blind tasting in which the subjects were actually blind. They were still blindfolded, and as an extra precaution, the wine glasses were completely black. With the color of the wine a mystery, they had to trust their other senses to deduce what was in the glass.

When I spoke to Trillin recently about this article, he mentioned that rosé had never come to mind. Instead, he performed these experiments with red and white only. Well, of course, I had to try it out myself. What if people couldn't actually tell the difference between the three colors? Perhaps their biases were all in their heads.

On an early October morning in New York City, I put this notion to the test. With a group of some of the best tasters around, I served them a combination of red, white, and rosé. The wine was served in black glasses and they were also blindfolded.

I used the same red wine that Trillin had used, a Pinot Noir from Sancerre. I also threw in two rosés, one light-bodied from Corsica and the other a bit fuller from California. For the white I served a more neutral but richer Chenin Blanc from California.

"It's funny how color affects your perception. I have never done this in my entire career," Jeff Porter, a seasoned professional who runs the beverage programs for Mario Batali's restaurants around the country, commented while tasting blind.

After all, in the early 1990s when Crystal Pepsi, a clear-white version of the popular soft drink, was released, people weren't having it. They had long associated the beverage with its brown color. Despite the similar flavor, people had serious trouble wrapping their head around a colorless version. People decided they didn't like it and the product failed.

While none of the sommeliers mistook the red wine for white or rosé, many had a hard time telling the difference between the white and rosé. Some even thought the California rosé was red.

Jane Lopes, a sommelier at the highly acclaimed Eleven Madison Park in New York City, added, "Rosé versus white wine is difficult. Red distinguishes itself more." She described rosé as "white wine with red fruit."

Others found comfort in being blindfolded. Ryan Totman, who works at Corkbuzz Wine Studio in New York City, who pushes himself daily in tasting and studying for sommelier tests, said, "You have growing pains going for all of these exams. It is nice when you can let the wines be 'anything.'"

There is certainly a sense of relief to be felt when you stop worrying about color. You have the opportunity to shed preconceptions and enjoy the wine for what it is, a delicious beverage.

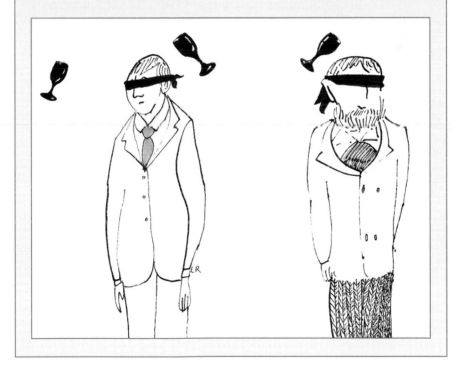

PEOPLE AND PLACES

Where the good stuff grows.

ROSÉ SETS DOWN ROOTS
GAINING A SENSE OF PLACE

Back in the day rosé was just rosé.
It didn't really matter. Now, there's typicity,
there's terroir, there are certain styles.

—RAJAT PARR

Twenty or thirty years ago you would walk into a restaurant and order a glass of house red. Now, you know where that red comes from. You have heard of Napa and you have heard of Bordeaux. You know what Cabernet Sauvignon tastes like. You know why you might or might not like it.

In the same way that we have become educated on red and white wine, rosé will follow. When I first started pouring a Corsican rosé by the glass at my restaurant, people were intrigued. Many had never had a wine from this French island and they were impressed by the quality.

Months later, I switched to a Loire Valley rosé. Guests who came in and ordered a glass of rosé, as they normally had, were taken aback. The wine tasted differently. Some loved the new pour and others disliked it.

Now, those same guests return and ask, "Do you still have the Loire rosé by the glass?" or "Is the Corsican rosé still being poured?" People have come to understand that just like any other wine, rosé has a taste that belongs to a sense of place.

As the category of pink wines grows, so do the number of drinkers who pay critical attention. People are concerned with producers and origin, which in turn will pressure producers to focus on quality. Gone are the days of ordering any pink swill the bar has.

REGIONS AND PRODUCERS
FAMOUS FOR ROSÉ

Rosé is made in almost every region where grapes are grown. With that many options, it's hard to know what's good and what's not. What follows is a breakdown of the most common places to find rosés and the people who produce them throughout the world. Included are the best rosés, the most important rosés, and my favorite rosés.

PROVENCE
The Birthplace of French Wine

No other region can boast the history that Provence holds with pink wine. The style has been made here before France was even France. Today, when people think of rosé, the Provençal style is usually what comes to mind. But be careful! A ton of pink bathwater is also made here. For the good stuff, you'll have to do a bit of searching on the shelves.

A lot of rosés here are bottled in the traditional, hourglass-shaped bottle known as a *skittle*. This might look and sound cool but it doesn't mean the wine is of any higher quality. Also, if something sounds gimmicky, it probably isn't worth drinking. Run when you see wine names that use words that are stuck in the 1990s like "angel" or "whisper."

Provence is a region that has struggled to supply demanding consumers while maintaining quality. At Domaine Triennes, Jeremy Seysses notes, "It is both tempting and easy to pick too late in a sunny region like Provence," but adds that they are "sticklers when it comes to the timing of harvest." This attention to detail is what separates quality-minded producers from bulk wineries.

Seysses adds, "We have grown a lot ourselves, conscious that this growth could not come at the expense of quality, but on the contrary, provide investment in order for us to gain access to better supply, better equipment, and help us grow in quality as well as volume. We now have better suppliers, better presses, and better temperature control than we had ten years ago."

When the wines from Provence are good, they're really good. Take, for example,

Domaine Hauvette. Near Saint-Rémy-de-Provence, where Van Gogh painted his famous *Starry Night*, the wines are just as captivating. Their rosé smells of garigue, the wild Mediterranean herbs that coat the countryside. These small vignerons demonstrate that Provence can still make great wine, even after 2,600 years.

GRAPES: Mostly Cinsault, Grenache, Mourvèdre, Syrah, and Tibouren, but also Ugni Blanc, Counoise, Clairette, Vermentino, Sémillon, Cabernet Sauvignon, and Carignan

FAVORITES: La Commanderie de Peyrassol, Domaine Triennes, Domaine Hauvette, Château de Roquefort, Domaine de Sulauze, and Clos Cibonne

CASSIS

Nestled within Provence, along the coast, this tiny region is oftentimes forgotten, but this is one of the most beautiful places you will ever see. Let a glass of wine transport you there, and as often as possible. The wines here use less Mourvèdre than neighboring Bandol, and therefore are less powerful, possessing less tannin. They also have lower levels of alcohol and are lighter in style. Overall, I like to think of the wines as Bandol's delicate cousins.

Highly drinkable, the wines gain salinity from the proximity to the sea. This iodine character makes them perfect for seafood dishes. Jonathan Sack-Zafiropulo of Clos Sainte Magdeleine explains that the ancient fishing village of Cassis is also famous for its unique limestone soil. His winery is actually located in the Les Calanques National Park, a breathtaking and steep limestone outcropping that rises out from the Mediterranean.

GRAPES: Mostly Cinsault, Grenache, and Mourvèdre, but also Bourboulenc, Clairette, Ugni Blanc, Sauvignon Blanc, Pascal Blanc, Marsanne, Barbaroux, Carignan, and Terret Noir

FAVORITES: Clos Sainte Magdeleine and Domaine du Bagnol

PALETTE

This tiny region in Provence is dominated by the exceptional Château Simone. There are five other wineries but quality is variable and the wines are not seen in stores very often. So why talk about a region when only one producer is of note? Once you try their rosé, you'll understand.

Château Simone has been in the hands of the Rougier family for two centuries. Their vineyards sit on limestone soils on the slopes of the Montaiguet Mountains. Some of their vines are over a century old—an extreme rarity. The older the vines, the more concentrated and, theoretically, the higher quality the fruit.

Before it was fashionable, they practiced organic viticulture, because it was "the right thing to do." You can sense this forward thinking in their wines. Jean François

Rougier has mentioned to me that organic is not a trend for them but rather a continuation of history. "Our rosé has not changed, we are faithful to our traditional practices."

Many argue that this is an example of a rosé that improves with age. Sommeliers and wine writers will brag that they have had ten- or twenty-year-old bottles that belied the notion of young consumption.

The Rougier family only exports small quantities of their wine to the United States, so if you see a bottle, snatch it up.

GRAPES: Mostly Grenache, Mourvèdre, and Cinsault, but also Brun Fourca, Cabernet Sauvignon, Carignan, Castet, Durif, Muscat de Hambourg, Muscat à Petits Grains Rouge, Petit Brun, Syrah, Téoulier, Terret Gris, Tibouren, and a lot of other lesser-known grapes

FAVORITE: Château Simone

BANDOL

Bandol, regarded as the "Grand Cru" of Provence, produces rosés using the Mourvèdre grape. This dark-ruby grape makes wines full of black fruit, purple flowers, garigue, and an overwhelming wild note usually described as earth, cured meats, and leather.

Lucien Peyraud, who began the Domaine Tempier winery, is the reason that Mourvèdre dominates in Bandol. He championed for the grape at a time when it was being ripped out and other varieties were being planted that produced higher yields—because more wine meant more money. Along with other vignerons, he established Bandol as its own region, within Provence.

Domaine Tempier has been a hub of the Provençal lifestyle since 1936. Just outside the seaport village of Bandol, culinary superstars like Richard Olney and Alice Waters spent time in Lulu Peyraud's (Lucien's wife) hearth kitchen. Creating magical lunches and suppers for hundreds, she focuses on traditional dishes like pisaldiere, bouillabaise, and olive tapenade. Today she is ninety-nine years old and still a firecracker, as are her wines.

Even in the 1970s in America, at a time when rosé was not popular, restaurants like the highly acclaimed Chez Panisse in Northern California poured Domaine Tempier rosé. Alice Waters, the innovative chef and owner of Chez Panisse has told me, "We were pretty open to anything that came from Domaine Tempier. We were such admirers and friends. I loved the color of the rosé and just thought what a beautiful way to welcome people into the restaurant. I started serving it to all of my friends."

Alice Waters met the Peyrauds in their home in Bandol in the 1970s with food writer Richard Olney. It was there that she fell in love with the Provençal lifestyle and gained inspiration for Chez Panisse. She spent her mornings going to the market with Lulu and in the Peyrauds' gardens. At night, around their dinner table, she fell in love with the family and the wines.

The wines, as Alice Waters noted, are very hard to separate from the family. They embody the Provençal lifestyle. They are in themselves an experience. When Kermit Lynch was looking into other rosés to import from France, he had a hard time finding anything similar. "I went around tasting so many rosés, but I wasn't finding the same quality as I was at Tempier. It took me awhile to figure out, to ask winemakers, how do you make your rosé? And then I found out that Domaine Tempier wasn't doing things like other people."

For one, they were making rosé for the sake of making rosé. It was not an accident or something they made from rotten grapes. Indeed, there was a special section of the vineyard that was always destined to make this wine. With care and precision they crafted it into a pink wine. When doing so, they also used indigenous yeasts, so it was truly a wine that tasted like the environment.

Some producers do this today, but more often than not, they will ship in manufactured yeasts. That is why so much wine tastes the same. It is not made from the natural yeasts that are found in the atmosphere—what naturally fermented wine for centuries.

Domaine Tempier also allows their rosés to go through both fermentations. A lot of wine goes through two fermentations—alcoholic fermentation and malolactic fermentation. You might think you don't want to get into the science of it, but I think it's pretty neat. Basically, after the sugar has been converted to alcohol, another fermentation naturally takes place. The malic acid (think Granny Smith apple—tart acidity) will transform to lactic acid (think a glass of milk—rounder acidity). This makes the

= Malic

= Lactic

Milk

Milk

HAVE YOU SEEN ME?

Name: Lactic Acid
Nickname: $CH_3CH(OH)$
  CO_2H
Last seen: In a solid
style: water-soluble

wine lusher and more supple. Almost all red wine goes through this process, but nowadays, only a handful of whites. Rosés, well, very few.

We didn't even know this second fermentation existed for the longest time. People picked their grapes and turned them into wine. But now, as science has caught up, a lot of winemakers are purposely blocking malolactic fermentation. "When you block the malolactic, you don't just tell it to stop, you have to do something to make it stop. Usually that is sterile filtration, and a good dose of sulfur dioxide," Kermit Lynch reports. These two things can really mess with a wine and make it taste mass-produced—soulless.

Tempier rosé has now gained cult status. Collectors will stash away cases to drink five to ten years later. Wineries in California like Railsback Fréres and Bedrock Wine Company have crafted rosés of a similar style as an ode to Lulu herself.

Within Bandol, you see a concentration of quality. Delve deep into the region and try as much rosé as you can find. Make sure to pair it with southern French cuisine that would make Lulu proud.

GRAPES: Mostly Mourvèdre, Cinsault, and Grenache, but also Bourboulenc, Carignan, Clairette, Syrah, and Ugni Blanc

FAVORITES: Domaine de Terrebrune, Domaine Tempier, Domaine du Gros Noré, Château Pibarnon, and Château Pradeaux

TAVEL
The Original "Brosé" Wine Was a Favorite Among
Ernest Hemingway and Kings

This is a wine of mythic proportions. It has been called the "Rosé of Kings" and the "King of Rosés" due to its fan club members—Louis XIV and Philippe IV just to name a couple. Situated in the Rhône valley in France, this region is almost exclusively dedicated to rosés.

The vineyards in Tavel soak up the summer heat. Without protective winds like the mistral, the grapes would bake. These hearty grapes hold a good bit of sugar resulting in wines with a bit more alcohol and body.

Here, winemakers tend to leave the grape juice in contact with the skins for a bit longer. This leads to a deeper color of rosé and a bit of tannin, allowing some wines to improve with age like those from Bandol. At times, I think this can be exaggerated. Still, tasting a bottle with a few years of age can be quite nice. Bruce Neyers, who does national sales for Kermit Lynch Wine Merchant, notes that the first rosé he remembers tasting (and enjoying) was a Tavel rosé in 1972.

Only a small bit of Tavel rosé actually makes it to the United States. Sadly, what does make it across the ocean is usually lower in quality. Make sure to stick to solid producers, like the ones listed below. Maybe stick a few in your wine cellar and forget about them. See what happens after a few years of bottle age.

GRAPES: Mostly Grenache, but also some Clairette, Cinsault, Mourvèdre, Piquepoul, Syrah, and Carignan

FAVORITES: Château de Trinquevedel, Domaine L'Anglore, and Domaine Moulin La Viguerie

CORSICA
France's Little Island with Fiercely Independent Winemakers

In general, there tend to be two styles of rosé, one heavier, denser and one lighter, crisp style. Corsican rosé is perfectly in the middle. It has richness but also is fresh and clean. Now it is my go-to rosé, there's nothing like it. Its pretty incredible how complex they are, how structured and rich. My favorite is probably from Clos Canarelli.

—RAJAT PARR

It's true. Rosés from Corsica can convert even the snobbiest of wine drinkers. I always sneak one in during a tasting menu at the restaurant. The guests, who already agreed to the wine pairing, might wince when they first see the color, but only empty glasses have been returned. One regular diner now comes back just to try the various Corsican rosés we pour with all of our dishes.

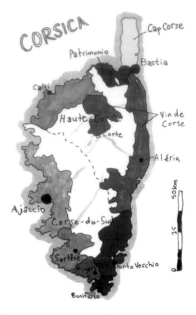

The rosés produced here are refreshingly innovative. Made usually from a mix of Spanish, French, and Italian grape varieties, they are not like mainland wines. A visit to the winery of Domaine Comte Abbatucci demonstrates this fact. Kermit Lynch and his notes online (see "Resources") will tell you that the estate is named after local French Revolutionary hero General Jean-Charles Abbatucci and friend of the most famous Corsican, Napoléon Bonaparte. Today, the estate is owned by Jean-Charles Abbatucci (a direct descendent of the General), who, like all islanders, is a proud defender of its traditions and its land.

Abbatucci has saved many ancient Corsican grape varieties from extinction, climbing high up into the mountains to source cuttings of old vines. A staunch advocate of biodynamics as well as the traditional Corsican polyphonic songs, he will blast the music through the vineyards claiming it "keeps the vines happy."

A bit farther north, in Patrimonio, Yves Leccia is a founding member of A Filetta, an apparently very famous Corsican polyphonic singing group. He also creates some of the most elegant and sophisticated wines on the island. His rosés focus on the Nielluccio grape, which is genetically related to Sangiovese. Indeed, these wines do share a similarity to their Tuscan relative, but have an expression that is entirely their own.

Far south, in the ancient growing region of Figari, Yves Canarelli at Clos Canarelli is a true pioneer. An intellectual and experimentalist, he has ripped out entire vineyards of foreign varieties and replanted them with native varieties. These painstaking, expensive actions have eventually paid off. Canarelli produces a symbol of what Corsican rosé can be—fiercely independent, vibrant, and precise.

CHAMPAGNE

A Mistake Led to One of the World's Most Expensive Styles of Rosé

In the Middle Ages, winemakers in Champagne created a *gris* style of wine, the result from pressing red grapes for white wine. Without modern technology, the juice naturally had a pink color to it. Some twisted person decided it looked like the eye of a partridge, bloodshot before its death. The disturbing name—Oeil de Perdrix—became the colloquial name for the rosé.

It has recently been discovered that the first Champagne house to sell rosé Champagne was Ruinart. A document from March 14, 1764, notes a sale of a batch of Oeil de Perdrix. The current Chef de Cave, Frédéric Panaïotis, speculates that this was probably an accident, perhaps a maceration that went a little too long.

Today, the vast majority of rosé Champagnes are made using blending. This is all thanks to the Veuve (Widow) Clicquot. When her husband passed in 1805, she took charge of their Champagne house, revolutionizing many techniques in the region. She particularly disliked rosé Champagne made by maceration. Through exhaustive experimentation she discovered that blending yielded the best results. This takes place prior to the second fermentation (where the bubbles are created). In 1818, she added still red wine to the cuvée. Higher-quality rosé Champagne was born.

In the latter part of the eighteenth century, the wine was nicknamed "rounceet" which eventually morphed into "rosé." The ancient term of Oeil de Perdrix is rarely seen anymore in Champagne. Doyard is the most notable house that still uses the term on the label.

Funnily enough, the name spread to Switzerland where today, in the canton of Neuchâtel, it is still a very popular name for dry rosé. Sadly, it is not exported to the

United States. The Swiss are very protective of their wines and did not take well to Bob Trinchero from Sutter Home stealing the name Oeil de Perdrix for the early White Zinfandel. They famously scoffed that this wine is for "blue-haired ladies."

Today, rosé Champagne is often considered one of the finest offerings in the wine world. It can be astronomically more expensive than its blanc counterparts. The process in creating pink versions can require more precision and is very time consuming. Since a bit of still red wine is usually added, the final product is considered more vinous, as in it tastes more like regular wine. The added still red wine also adds tannin, giving it a bit more structure and the ability to hold up to age well.

Even though this is a pricey beverage, affordable options exist that are incredibly tasty. Options from growers can be very value-driven. Look for a little "RM" on the label; this means it was made by a farmer, not a big company.

Rosé Champagne is one of the most versatile wines in the world, going with any food and any occasion. I highly suggest drinking it throughout dinner.

GRAPES: Mostly Pinot Noir, Chardonnay, and Pinot Meunier, but also Pinot Blanc, Pinot Gris, Arbane, and Petit Meslier

FAVORITES: Marc Hebrart, Doyard, Paul Bara, R. Geoffroy, Henri Billiot, Jean Lallement, Chartogne-Taillet, Billecart-Salmon, Jacques Selosse, Krug, Ruinart, J. Lassalle, Veuve Fourny, Pehu Simonet, Varnier-Fanniere, Le Chapitre, Billecart-Salmon, La Caravelle, Egly Ouriet, and Gaston Chiquot

ROSÉ DES RICEYS

A rare find, but this is still a rosé made in the Champagne region. You might not come across a bottle of this whimsical wine in your lifetime. But if you do, it's worth checking out. Here, Pinot Noir, from farther south in the Aube region of Champagne, is crafted into a still rosé. The wine has been made since the 1100s by Cistercian Monks. Like in Burgundy, these monks studied where the snow would first melt in the spring. There, on southern-facing hillsides, they planted Pinot Noir. Pinot Noir can have trouble ripening this far north, so if it can't be successfully made into this beautifully aromatic rosé, it is instead sold off to make Champagne.

Only about twenty producers make Rosé des Riceys. You might be able to find it in a wine bar in Paris, but even then, good luck. Even Louis XIV, who is said to have discovered this wine, had to have special shipments sent to him from Riceys. Most collectors today make an annual pilgrimage to the region to stock up for the year.

No other wine region boasts regulations as strict for rosé as here. Steeped in tradition, the proud growers are staunch advocates of producing the expressive and delicate wine properly or not at all. It must be produced by the saignée method and the grapes must be picked at a specific level of ripeness from vines that are at least twelve years old.

Should you come across the wine in your travels, make sure to give it a shot. Besides being delicious, it is an emblem of commitment to tradition.

THE LOIRE VALLEY
The Garden of France

This area follows France's longest river, the Loire. It stretches from the Atlantic coast all the way to central vineyards around Sancerre, just two hours south of Paris. Almost every subregion within the Loire Valley produces a rosé of some kind, ranging from rustic to whimsical. The amount of grapes and styles is enough to make anyone lose their balance. Just breathe in and explore a bit at a time.

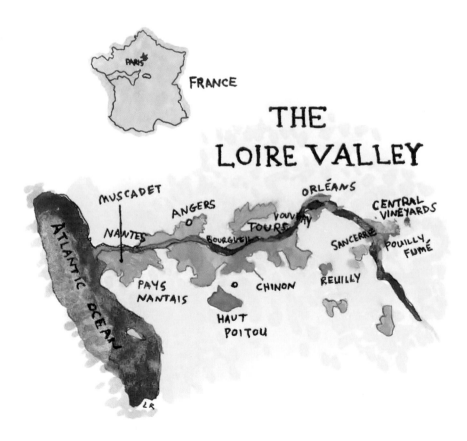

PÉT-NAT

A recent resurgence of an ancient tradition is *pétillant naturel* (pét-nat or naturally sparkling wines). These wines are fun, slightly fizzy, and ideal for picnics. They are *glou-glou* wines, the kind you want to gulp-gulp. Think of soda pop but with alcohol. New York wine writer Zachary Sussman writes about the trend:

> One is left with the curious impression that pét-nat represents two contradictory things: on the one hand, it's the latest hipster-approved wine trend—the kind of effortlessly drinkable stuff designed to be knocked back with abandon. And yet, on the other, it's designed to be some sort of old-school vinous throwback steeped in tradition.

These wines are made in a method that pre-dates Champagne known as "ancestral." When wine is made, carbon dioxide is always naturally produced. Usually, it disappears and escapes into the air, so you don't notice it. However, in this method, the winemaker traps the carbon dioxide in a wine bottle, so there is a natural fizziness leftover. There is usually a bit of residual sugar and the yeast cells, once exhausted from their duties, fall gently to the bottom of the bottle. Don't be alarmed by the slight sweetness or cloudy appearance, just embrace it.

REUILLY PINOT GRIS
The Fancy Kind of Pinot Grigio

Here Pinot Grigio goes by its French name, Pinot Gris. In Northern Italy, they allow color from the skins to enter the wine, resulting in a naturally pink wine from a technically white grape. In Reuilly they do the same. Winemakers like Denis Jamain make a rosé from Pinot Gris, resulting in a fresh and slightly colored wine.

SANCERRE AND CHINON

The most famous rosés of the Loire Valley historically come from Sancerre and Chinon. In Sancerre, due to the soil and proximity to Champagne and Burgundy, the wines are similarly based on Pinot Noir. In Chinon, farther west, you find more Bordeaux varieties. Cabernet Franc and Cabernet Sauvignon in particular make up the majority of rosés in Chinon. Winemakers like Rodolphe Raffault of Domaine Jean-Maurice Raffault are spearheading the quality movement.

After studying in Burgundy, Raffault continues to follow in his father's footsteps, making wines with careful precision. For rosé, he selects grapes from parcels with silt, sand, and gravel soil. Unlike other winemakers in the region, where rosé is not a priority, he focuses on quality every year. He says, "For my winery, I always vinify this wine like a serious wine, I use the same method for rosé that I use for the white wine."

Move a bit east and you will find yourself in Sancerre. Here, Pinot Noir takes center stage. These are similar to the rare Rosé des Riceys that you find in the South of Champagne. Lean and racy with pretty red fruit aromatics, they are some of the most sought-after pink wines on the market.

François Cotat is one of the legends of Sancerre. He only makes a few bottles of rosé and very little of it makes it to the United States. The wine itself is hard to describe, so I would call it simple yet fulfilling.

Why are these cult wines so captivating? David Hinkle of Skurnik wines told me, "Winemakers visited, but there are zero that [Cotat] can transmit. It has to do with the vineyards, the cellar. There is no simple takeaway."

If you cannot find Cotat rosé, not to worry. There are plenty of delicious Pinot Noir rosés produced. Vacheron makes tasty pink wines. So do many others like Daniel Chotard and Domaine Hippolyte Reverdy. The beauty of the Loire Valley is that there are so many styles of rosé outside of Sancerre and Chinon. Try one from Bourgueil or Cheverney. Look for fun grapes like Grolleau, Pineau d'Aunis, and Cot. This is the place to experiment, at a price point that makes it easy to do so.

GRAPES: Mainly Pinot Noir, Cabernet Franc, Cabernet Sauvignon, Pinot Gris, Pinot Meunier, Gamay, Cot (Malbec), Pineau d'Aunis, and Grolleau

---

FAVORITES: François Cotat, Pascal Cotat, Daniel Chotard, Domaine Vacheron, Domaine Roger Neveu, Domaine Hippolyte Reverdy, Domaine du Salvard, Domaine de Reuilly, Bernard Baudry, Catherine & Pierre Breton, Domaine de la Chanteleuserie, J. M. Raffault, Charles Joguet, and Olga Raffault

Rosé

CHINON

appellation contrôlée

SCEA CHARLES JOGUET
VITICULTEUR à SAZILLY (37220) - FR
WWW.CHARLESJOGUET.com

Mis en bouteille au domaine

2016

IMPORTED BY
KERMIT LYNCH WINE MERCHANT
BERKELEY, CALIFORNIA

ALC. 12.5% BY VOL.
ROSE CHINON WINE

750ML
PRODUCT OF FRANCE

ITALY
Cerasuolo "Cherry Red" Wines from Abruzzo

This wine's cherry red color comes from a bit of contact with the Montepulciano grape skins. Although many producers in the Abruzzo region produce a cerasuolo, only one man has created a legend. Edoardo Valentini is an exception in a region known for bulk and bland wines. A recluse, he never gave any details on how his wine was made, except that he used large, old oak casks. There was no website to visit and he was never reachable by email. In 2006, he passed, leaving the estate to his son  Francesco. When an importer approached Francesco about representing his wines in the United States, his infamous response was, "You have to write me a letter, by hand." The apple did not fall far from the tree.

Many have told me that his mysterious methods can only be guessed, as the wine is like no other rosé you have ever tasted. To my knowledge, it is also the most expensive still rosé on the market. Little of this wine is made and even less comes to the United States. I knew I had to find out more. After some failed attempts (and some clever workarounds) I finally received an email back.

His family has been making wine in Abruzzo since the 1800s. Nothing has changed. They still use the same barrels and make the wine as they always have. "In the artisanal process, there are no schemes or protocols to follow. You follow the experience and the sensations. The emotional and intuitive component are much more important than the rational one. I consider Cerasuolo (Abruzzo rosé) different from other Italian rosés," he began, adding in that structure, good alcohol levels and great acidity were important. These are the things you won't find elsewhere. He brings the red grapes into the winery and presses them right away. "I think that in a rosé, even only a short skin maceration could let the wine lose those main characteristics of a rosé, such as freshness, floral and fruit flavors. Therefore if you let the wine spend time with the skins, it will get closer to a red wine."

What makes his wine so special is his natural approach. The yeasts are all indigenous, nothing is temperature controlled, there is no filtering, and all big wooden casks are used—essentially it is a wine that is not tampered with. This cannot last forever, though. Due to global warming, he told me that he will "stop his vinifications." He describes his wines as artisanal products that are obtained without the help of technology, so the correct ripening and evolution of the grape is of fundamental importance. He has noticed that with the climate change, the sugar and the phenolic ripening is not what it used to be. Abruzzo is a warm place and it is now getting too warm.

Francesco finds it of utmost importance to "respect Mother Nature, with her balance and harmonies." When climate change accelerates, he won't be able to correct his grapes (and ultimately, his wines) with technology. That would be against his philosophy.

Cerasuolo is one of the most versatile rosés you can find. Due to the power and elevated acidity, the wine can go with dishes other pink wines are too delicate for. Even Francesco could not resist mentioning all of the foods he loves with the wine. "I consider the Cerasuolo to be a wine particularly suitable for food. It can be easily paired with pastas with a filling sauce (like meat ragù), or with fish (fish soup or grilled fish) or also can be paired to a good pizza." Make sure to try these wines while he still makes them.

There are a few other excellent producers in this region as well. It is a region that has yet to be fully appreciated, though. America is just starting to see some of the best wines from here. In a moment of optimism, Francesco notes, "Regarding the future of wine in Abruzzo, I see it as very good, or to stay in theme, I'd call it rosy."

GRAPE: Montepulciano

FAVORITES: Edoardo Valentini, Edmidio Pepe, Praesidium, Annona, and Tiboiro

Naturally Pink Pinot Grigio

Pinot Grigio is one of the few white grapes that has color in its skin. The skins are slightly copper pink. If pressed right away, it is hard to see any color in the wine, but with a bit of skin contact, the wine can pick up beautiful pink hues. This practice is common in Friuli in Northern Italy, near Venice. Here the wine is called ramato, which translates to "auburn."

Pre-1970s, this style of wine was common for Pinot Grigio. This was when they didn't have a lot of modern technology like stainless steel tanks and fancy presses, so there was no way to avoid this slight rosé color. The wine picked up a ton of aromatic compounds from the skins, giving it much more complexity. The only problem was, it also picked up a good bit of tannin from the skins. This is fine for red wine, but people often found it too bitter and not refreshing for a Pinot Grigio.

Today, producers like Giampaolo Venica, have perfected the art of making delicious Pinot Grigio. This innovative winemaker uses modern technology to create a more traditional style. They use a press that is connected to a balloon filled with carbon dioxide. This protects the wine from turning brown and oxidizing, therefore it is a fresher and stronger color that he describes as "very orange, almost like Aperol." By avoiding long macerations at a very cold temperature, there is also no bitterness in the final product, just a pretty, pink, refreshing wine.

So why does Venica make Pinot Grigio this way? He says it is to prove a point: "When I started twenty years ago, [Pinot Grigio] was a shitty, watery thing. People would not try mine because they said it was too perfumed, colorful, and flavorful."

Pinot Grigio can taste delicious. Venica goes through the painstaking process of making sure this happens even before the grapes get to the winery. In the vineyard, he makes sure the vines are low-yielding and therefore produce more concentrated grapes. There is no fining or filtering or a ton of sulfites added. He wants the wine to taste like a place—like the lake it is named after and that the vines overlook. "Pinot Grigio," he adds, "it has a meaning to it."

GRAPE: Pinot Grigio

FAVORITES: Venica & Venica and Dario Princic

Friuli

Trieste

Venice

MILAN

Florence

Abruzzo

Rome

ITALY

SICILY

AUSTRIA
Schilcher, a Historic Specialty in the South of Austria, Drives People "Rabid"

> *I think it is good for fat and heavy food. The acidity can handle that*
> *quite well and the light alcohol is a good contrast to that. Or just to*
> *drink a glass on sunny summer days.*
> —SEPP MUSTER, WINEMAKER

In 400 BCE, the Celtics selected the Wildbacher variety from local grapes in the region to make into wine. The grape was called *Rabiatperle* meaning "rabid pearl." Those who drank the wine turned rabid with intoxication. My guess is they might have overdone it a bit.

The wine later gained the name *Schilcher*, which was first noted around 1580 in a book from Johann Rasch. The word is a form of *schiller*, which means "to shine between red and white." One of the earliest rosés!

According to winemaker Franz Strohmeier, Wildbacher was originally made into a light pink wine because "of the late ripeness and the higher acid, making it a better rosé than a red." A specialty only of Styria, the style gained hype in the 1990s. Today, this distinct rosé is made into still, sparkling, and sweet wines. My favorites are the dry and sometimes slightly sparkling examples. Many are made in a more natural style. Overall, these are highly drinkable wines to enjoy with sauerkraut, pretzels, and rosé soup (see "Rosé Recipes" for the recipe).

GRAPE: Blauer Wildbacher

FAVORITES: Franz Strohmeier and Weingut Maria & Sepp Muster

OTHER OLD WORLD ROSÉ

Outside of the highlighted regions, there are so many wonderful examples of rosé being produced. Listed in no particular order is a shout-out to some of my favorite producers making tasty pink wine in other Old World countries.

AUSTRIA: Nigl (Kremstal), Schlosskellerei Gobelsburg Cistercien Niederösterreich (Kamptal), Loimer (Niederösterreich), Weingut Jäger (Wachau), and Emmerich Knoll (Wachau)

BASQUE COUNTRY: Ameztoi Rubentis Getariako Txakolina and Ulacia Getariako Txakolina

FRANCE: Renardat-Fâche Bugey-Cerdon (Savoie), Patrick Bottex Bugey-Cerdon (Savoie), Bruno Clair Marsannay (Burgundy), Domaine Migot Vins Gris (Lorraine), Maxime Magnon (Corbières), Domaine de Fontsainte (Corbières), Domaine d'Aupilhac (Languedoc), Domaine la Tour Vieille (Collioure), Mas de Daumas Gassac (Languedoc), and Domaine Les Pallières (Gigondas)

GERMANY: Stein (Mosel), Messmer (Pfalz), Rebholz (Pfalz), von Buhl (Pfalz), Leitz (Rheingau), and Schlossgut Diel (Nahe)

SWITZERLAND: Domaine de Montmollin Oeil de Perdrix (Neuchâtel) and Château d'Auvernier Oeil de Perdrix (Neuchâtel)

NEW WORLD ROSÉ

Outside of Europe, winemakers are embracing rosé and playing with their own styles. The United States is one such place. The American palate is starting to evolve. Winemakers have a growing appreciation for rosé and are further exploring the style. Rosé has sparked a wave of excitement and experimentation. In California, winemakers like Rajat Parr are playing with fractional blending. Three different vintages of rosé (2012, 2013, and 2014) are aged in the solera method, something more commonly found in sherry production. In this method, a bit of each vintage is blended and aged together. It will be released as a sparkling wine in 2017.

In Oregon, J. K. Carriere is making Pinot Noir rosé with Chardonnay lees, the expended yeast cells. Usually, these settle to the bottom of the tank and can be discarded. By adding it to another wine, they are adding a clever twist to Pinot Noir and Chardonnay usage, two of the traditional grapes incorporated into champagne made in France. Eventually the wine is separated and bottled, but not before picking up some flavor and a silky texture from the Chardonnay lees.

In New York, Macari Vineyards on the North Fork of Long Island makes a delicious rosé that sells out every vintage. Nearby, Paumanok also makes a highly quaffable example from Bordeaux varieties. Since there are no traditional grapes associated with a region, wineries are playing around and seeing what works best. In

Santa Ynez Valley in California, Lieu Dit is committed to only Loire Valley varieties, for example. Their rosé is made from Pinot Noir and is reminiscent of Sancerre rosés but with its own California stamp.

In Sonoma, Soliste winery also makes a Pinot Noir rosé. The market is still tricky for pink wines, though. The owner of the winery, Claude Koeberle, has told me that he makes rosé because he likes it, not because he wants to make a profit. He cannot command as high of a price point for it as he can his red wine made from Pinot Noir. "Every time we sell a bottle of rosé, we actually lose 75 cents."

Consumers are slowly starting to embrace New World examples of rosé and will hopefully explore options from around the globe. Australia, Chile, South Africa, Canada, New Zealand, and many other countries are now making world-class pink wine.

As a broad sweeping statement, New World rosés tend to offer a more fruit profile versus a mineral one. Due to more sun exposure and warmer conditions, they often have a higher alcohol content, making them full-bodied. These rosés can also be much more aromatic in comparison to their Old World counterparts.

GRAPES: A wide range of varieties

FAVORITES: Macari, Paumanok, Lieu Dit, Railsback Frères, Jolie-Laide, Bedrock, Wine Co., Idlewild, J. K. Carriere, Arnot Roberts, Soliste, and Presqu'ile

WHY AND HOW TO DRINK PINK

THE VERSATILITY OF ROSÉ

Kermit Lynch once described rosé as "red wine without tannins." Indeed, the drink can have a lot of the aromatics and fruit of a good red. The difference is in the structure. Tannin in wine originates from the skins, seeds, and stems of grapes. It also comes from oak, so if the wine spent time in new barrels, it will have a bit of this extract as well. These two types of tannins are logically found in many reds—but not in rosés. Tannins also provide that drying effect in your mouth. With some foods, they are great, like fatty meats that need the drying component to break through the richness. With other foods, like oily fish, they are a disaster. The tannins in reds react with the oil to produce a bitter, almost metallic taste on the palate. So when you want to avoid the messiness that tannins can cause with some dishes, order pink wine.

The grapes used for rosés are usually picked a bit earlier than those destined for reds (and sometimes whites) to preserve the freshness of the wine, the acidity. This refreshing element is able to cut through fatty dishes and clean your palate. As a result, rosés are excellent alongside briny dishes like anchovies and oysters.

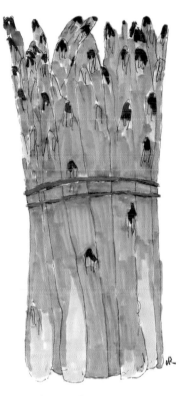

So, what separates rosés from whites? The texture and aromatics are what separates them. The bit of skin contact and color that is picked up in a rosé allows for much more versatility in pairings. Winemaker Giampaolo Venica from Friuli, a region in northeast Italy, adds that rose is perfect for traditional dishes where white wine just doesn't cut it, like in spring, when white and green asparagus is in season. Served with a sauce of boiled, crushed eggs and vinegar, the broadness of his Pinot Grigio, which sees a bit of skin contact and picks up color, is a perfect accompaniment for the dish.

In Chinon, a town in the Loire Valley in France, asparagus is also paired with rosé. Winemaker Rodolphe Raffault of Jean-Maurice Raffault gleams, "Often, I serve for my friends cooked white asparagus (from sandy soils of the Loire Valley) with a spicy mayonnaise sauce (my own recipe, with Espelette pepper and Black Malabar pepper)." While dishes with heavy pepper spice and vegetal components can overpower some whites, rosés pair perfectly.

ROSÉ ALL DAY AND ALL YEAR

I was in a restaurant in New York, about three years ago, with my wife
and two kids. With them, as is usual these days, everybody ordered
something different. I thought, "My God! Oh…let's have rosé!" The
sommelier said, "So sorry, it's November. We don't offer rosé during the
winter." I thought that was one of the oddest things I had ever heard. I
had never imagined someone might think like that. One of the pleasures
of rosé is that it would have gone well with everything we ordered.

—KERMIT LYNCH

Why do we think that rosé should be banned only to the warmer months? It is as silly as only drinking Champagne for celebrations. Over time, we have come to associate rosé just with summer—and it is about time we stopped! The beauty of rosé is its versatility—how it straddles the line between red and white. It is the perfect pairing for many foods (tapas, cocktail spreads, main dishes)—all year long.

FAVORITE PAIRINGS BY CHEFS, SOMMELIERS, AND FOODIES

"In the summer, I will have friends over for an evening,
to play boule and for dinner. We will drink probably 110 bottles
of wine—almost half are rosé! Cheese, salami, prosciutto,
pâté, and salad go well . . . all of those summer things."

—JACQUES PÉPIN

"I just drink it almost all throughout the meal. I drink it almost every day.
For me, I think it just marries with all the food from Provence. Perhaps a fish
soup or even in a something like a chicken with garlic. It's very adaptable."

—ALICE WATERS,
owner of Chez Panisse, chef, activist, and author

"I love rosé because it pairs well with everything. Barbecue chicken,
orzo, summer . . . and bad decisions."

—JOSHUA "THE FAT JEW" OSTROVSKY,
plus-size male model, EDM tribute artist, rosé vintner

"I love the South of France and Mediterranean dishes,
especially grilled summer vegetables with herbs, garlic, and spices,
and rosé is always the perfect pair!"

— DANIEL BOULUD,
chef/owner, The Dinex Group

"Rosé works well with tapas, like anchovy toasts and tapenade.
But I never really think much about the perfect marriage.
Except with my wife, of course. If I'm in the mood for rosé,
I'll drink it no matter what's on the plate."

—KERMIT LYNCH

"Rosé with shellfish and raw marinated fish like crudo and
ceviche can be great. But you can also do something richer,
like beef carpaccio with a Marsannay rosé. I love Corsica and they
have some amazing charcuterie. . . . Sitting outside there, in the sun
with a little rosé, yeah, that would work well too."

—RAJAT PARR

"Rosé is perfect with any kind of charcuterie and cured meats.
The saltiness of the meat is lifted and softened by
the juicy fruit and subtle grip of the rosé."

—JANE LOPES,
sommelier, Eleven Madison Park

"While it might seem cliché, I really like to match rosé with foods with pink colors: salmon, tuna tartare, and seasonal tomatoes. Also, I find it's one of the few styles of wine that shines with eggs. Try a medium-bodied dry version with an herb and cheese frittata."

—GEOFF KRUTH,
master sommelier, COO Guild of Sommeliers

"Sautéed calamari."

—BRUCE NEYERS,
director of national sales, Kermit Lynch Wine Merchant

"My favorite time to drink rosé is with my family, preferably during an outdoor crab feast down in Maryland."

—DUSTIN WILSON,
master sommelier, co-founder Verve Wine

"Rosé is my happy place, any season, anytime, it always makes me smile and enjoy life more . . . and it's great with barbeque."

—JEFF PORTER,
beverage director at Batali & Bastianich Hospitality Group

"My favorite foods to eat with rosé are quite simple: Spanish white anchovies, grilled sardines, charcuterie, or a simple green salad. Beyond that, rosé pairs perfectly with a warm, sunny afternoon in the backyard with some Zydeco on the record player and burgers on the grill."

—ERIC HASTINGS,
beverage manager, Jean-Georges restaurants

"For pairings, I like when it is . . . not classic. Do not hesitate to add a bit of wildness to the pairing. Play with spices."

—OLIVIER KRUG,
director de la maison, Krug Champagne

"I love almost anything grilled with rosé but my go-to favorite dish is grilled sausages, hot and sweet."

—DANIEL JOHNNES,
wine director, Daniel Boulud's Dinex Group, and founder, La Paulée de New York

"Rosé can be paired with a wide range of foods depending on the weight and style, from a great cheeseburger with all of the fixings to oysters."

—CARRIE LYN STRONG,
wine director, Aureole, New York

"I tend to drink most of my rosé outdoors, when the sun is out and it is warm. As much as anything, it is a wine that I pair with weather. . . . It is very versatile and a joy to drink with salads and grilled fish in a Mediterranean style. I also like pairing it as I would Riesling, which is to say with spice as well as sweet and sour foods."

—JEREMY SEYSSES,
winemaker/owner, Domaine Dujac, Burgundy and Domaine de Triennes, Provence

". . . a fresh seafood platter near the sea!"

—RODOLPHE RAFFAULT,
Domaine Jean-Maurice Raffault, Chinon, Loire Valley, France

"When rosé begins to age a little, it can be married with a larger assortment of dishes: white meat, fish, shellfish, and old cheese. My personal preference is for grilled lobster."

—ETIENNE PORTALIS,
Château Pradeaux, Bandol, France

"My mother-in-law makes this amazing rock lobster with a spicy tomato sauce, that, with rosé, is delicious."

—DANIEL RAVIER,
Domaine Tempier, Bandol, France

ROSÉ
RECIPES

ROSÉ COCKTAILS

SURE, ROSÉ IS GREAT ON ITS OWN. NOW TRY THROWING IT into a cocktail. Your new favorite pink drink might have a little whiskey or perhaps some seasonal fruit. The versatility and wide array of rosé styles make the options endless.

Unless otherwise noted, each of the following recipes yields one cocktail. Get ready to muddle, mix, and serve up some tricks.

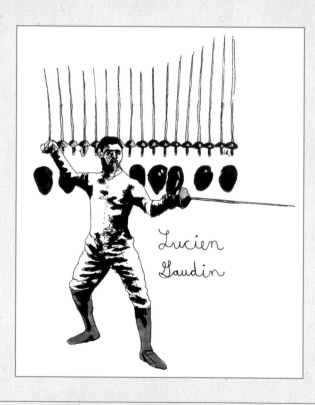

Lucien
Gaudin

ROSÉ LUCIEN GAUDIN

Named for an early twentieth century French Olympic fencer, the Lucien Gaudin is a celebratory twist on a classic bitter aperitif. This rendition uses rosé instead of vermouth.

1 OZ PLYMOUTH GIN

1 OZ LILLET* ROSÉ

½ OZ CAMPARI

½ OZ COINTREAU

2 DASHES OF GRAPEFRUIT BITTERS

ICE CUBES

1 ORANGE TWIST

Pour ingredients over a few cubes of ice and stir for two minutes or until chilled. Strain into a coupe glass. Dress with an orange twist.

*Lillet is an aromatized wine from France. You can substitute with any aromatized wine.

HOW TO EXTRACT OILS FROM CITRUS PEELS

A nifty little trick that will make you look like a professional bartender, extracting oils from a peel is actually quite simple. Take a sliced peel and with the skin side facing the cocktail, gently squeeze the edges. This will release a small mist of oils. The smell is amazing, coating the surface of the drink.

FROSÉ

A great way to cool down in the summer. Rosé is blended with seasonal fruits for a constantly evolving and refreshing drink.

---

1 CUP SEASONAL FRUIT, DICED (CITRUS IN WINTER, MELONS IN SPRING, BERRIES IN SUMMER, ORCHARD FRUIT IN FALL)

1 BOTTLE OF TXAKOLI ROSADO*

6 OZ AGAVE

LEMON OILS FROM ONE PEEL

Clean the fresh fruit and remove any stems or leaves, and dice. Freeze the fruit in a plastic bag overnight. Fill about 2 empty ice cube trays with rosé and also freeze overnight. The next day, place the wine ice cubes and frozen fruit in a blender and add agave. Blend until it has a smooth consistency. Serve in a rocks glass and garnish with lemon oil.

---

*Txakoli is a type of wine from the Basque region. You can use another fruit-driven style of rosé as a substitute.

SPREZZATURA

This Negroni Sbagliato-style cocktail comes from head bartender and craftsman Kenneth Vanhooser at Piora.

---

1 LARGE ICE CUBE

1 1/2 OZ WHITE RUM

1 OZ SWEET VERMOUTH

1 OZ CAMPARI

SPARKLING ROSÉ

1 ORANGE PEEL FOR GARNISH

In a rocks glass, add the rum, vermouth, and Campari over a large ice cube. Stir a few times. Top with a bit of sparkling rosé. Garnish with a large orange peel twist.

Sprezzatura

(n.) the ability to make one's actions seem effortless or to disguise one's true desire, feeling, or meaning.

(n.) studied carelessness.

(n.) a delicious cocktail finished with sparkling rosé.

ROSÉ PUNCH

Great for parties or large groups, this no-fuss recipe transforms simple ingredients into a tasty libation.

LEMONADE PUNCH CUBES

½ CUP LEMON JUICE, FRESHLY SQUEEZED

½ CUP SIMPLE SYRUP

¾ CUP WATER

FRESH CLOVER FLOWERS (OR ANY PRETTY EDIBLE FLOWER)

PUNCH

2 BOTTLES CHILLED BUGEY CERDON ROSÉ*

1 CUP BRANDY

1 CUP GRAPEFRUIT JUICE

⅛ CUP SIMPLE SYRUP

2 GRAPEFRUITS, CUT INTO THIN ROUNDS

½ CUP STRAWBERRIES, SLICED

½ CUP RASPBERRIES

2 LEMONS, CUT INTO THIN ROUNDS

2 CUPS COLD SPARKLING WATER

PUNCH CUBES: The day before, mix together the juice, simple syrup, and water. Pour mix into ice trays and place 2–3 clover flowers in each compartment. Freeze overnight.

PUNCH: In a large bowl, combine the wine, brandy, grapefruit juice, and simple syrup. Add the grapefruit, strawberries, raspberries, and lemon, and refrigerate until well chilled, about one hour. Remove from the refrigerator and add the sparkling water. Serve in cups over punch cubes.

---

*Bugey Cerdon is a slightly sweet sparkling wine made by ancestral method. Another off-dry slightly sparkling wine can take its place.

Rosé punch

ROSÉ REVIVER #2

A rendition of the Corpse Reviver #2, which was invented at London's Savoy Hotel by Harry Craddock to "revive your corpse" from a hangover. This rosé version is gentle and herbaceous.

¾ OZ COCCHI AMERICANO ROSA*

¾ OZ PLYMOUTH GIN

¾ OZ COINTREAU

¾ OZ LEMON JUICE

1 DASH ABSINTHE

ICE

1 ORANGE PEEL FOR OILS AND GARNISH

Stir ingredients together with ice and strain into a coupe glass. Garnish with orange oil and a twist.

---

*This is an Italian aromatized wine. You can substitute it with Lillet Rosé or something similar.

rosé reviver #2

ROSÉ AND SAND

A rendition of the classic Blood and Sand cocktail named after the 1922 film of the same name. This drink is perfect for beach days (or days when you wish you were at the beach).

1 OZ ROSÉ VERMOUTH
(BELSAZAR)*

1 OZ GLENLIVET, 12-YEAR-OLD

1 OZ CHERRY HEERING LIQUEUR

1 OZ ORANGE JUICE

ICE

1 LARGE ORANGE WEDGE FOR
GARNISH

Mix the ingredients together and shake until chilled. Strain over ice and garnish with an orange wedge.

*This is an aromatized wine from the Baden, Germany. It can be substituted with other rosé vermouths.

rosé & sand

DISCO QUEEN

This cocktail is from Jillian Vose, who mixes it up at the Dead Rabbit in New York City. It is the perfect mix of sweet and sour.

1/4 OZ GINGER SIMPLE SYRUP

3/4 OZ RASPBERRY SIMPLE SYRUP

1 DASH ABSINTHE

3/4 OZ LEMON JUICE

1/2 OZ GRAPEFRUIT JUICE

1/2 OZ COCCHI AMERICANO ROSA

1 1/2 OZ PLANTATION 3 STAR RUM

To make the simple syrups, combine equal parts water and sugar and bring to a boil. Infuse one batch with freshly grated ginger and another with fresh raspberries. You can muddle these into the warm mixture for more intensity. Once cool, strain the ginger and raspberries out.

Shake all of the ingredients together until chilled, and strain into a coupe glass. No garnish necessary.

ROSÉ CHAMPAGNE COCKTAIL

A celebratory and charming drink, perfect for New Year's Eve or a simple weekend brunch.

1 SUGAR CUBE

GRAPEFRUIT BITTERS

4 OZ ROSÉ CHAMPAGNE*

1 GRAPEFRUIT PEEL FOR GARNISH

Place a sugar cube in a Champagne flute and add four dashes of grapefruit bitters. Once dissolved, slowly pour in the Champagne. Stop a few inches from the rim of the glass. Garnish with a grapefruit twist.

*Rosé Champagne can be swapped out for a cheaper alternative, such as a Crémant.

ROSÉ SELTZER

A nifty little trick to keep things light during the summer. The rosé ice cubes slowly melt into the cocktail, keeping you hydrated with seltzer while simultaneously enjoying rosé.

ROSÉ CUBES

1 BOTTLE OF SANCERRE ROSÉ*

1 CUP OF ORGANIC CRANBERRY JUICE

SELTZER MIX

SPARKLING WATER

1 LEMON CUT INTO WEDGES FOR GARNISH

ROSÉ CUBES: Mix together the rosé and cranberry juice. Fill ice cube trays and let freeze overnight.

SELTZER: The next day, drop a few cubes in a highball glass and top with sparkling water. Wait 5–10 minutes before drinking. Serve with an extra side of sparkling water and a lemon wedge.

---

*Sancerre can be substituted with another lean and racy style of rosé, such as Chinon or Reuilly.

rosé seltzer

OOM PAH-PAH

This drink was featured on the Dead Rabbit Grocery and Grog's 2015 summer menu and was created by Long Thai. I always love it when you don't have to decide between tequila and rosé.

1 OZ FORTALEZA TEQUILA BLANCO

1 OZ LILLET ROSÉ

½ OZ CLEAR CREEK EAU DE VIE DE POMME

½ OZ COMBIER PAMPLEMOUSSE ROSE LIQUEUR

2 DASHES BITTERMENS HOPPED GRAPEFRUIT BITTERS

1 DASH BOKER'S BITTERS

ICE

1 GRAPEFRUIT PEEL FOR OIL AND GARNISH

Stir the ingredients together with ice and strain into a Nick & Nora martini glass (or coupe glass). Garnish with a grapefruit peel and oil.

Take note that while it might not taste like it, this is a boozy cocktail. One or two could get the best of you!

ROSÉ IN COOKING

ROSÉ GOES FAR BEYOND THE GLASS.

Spend an afternoon cooking octopus with olives and celery, and invite some friends over. Hang out in the warm kitchen, stirring the pot, and sipping a glass of Bandol rosé (make sure you have a few bottles). The aromas will transport you to the South of France.

The beauty of rosé is its versatility—nearly any type will go with these recipes. Incorporate a little rosé in the cooking, or simply leave it to enjoy with the finished dish. Either way, these recipes are a collection of my favorite things to eat with pink wine.

SNACKS
AND SIDES

WHETHER YOU ARE WAITING FOR SUPPER OR SIMPLY FEELING peckish, these are the perfect small bites. The recipes that follow are staples you can whip up in no time. Serve these during cocktail hour or at a picnic. Either way, your companions will be charmed by the simple sophistication of them.

RADISHES WITH BUTTER

I believe it is a requirement in France to enjoy a glass of rosé with this snack. The only trick to making this dish delicious is by sourcing the best ingredients possible.

---

1 BUNDLE FRESH RADISHES

5—6 TABLESPOONS OF BEURRE DE BARATTE*

1 FRESH BAGUETTE

1—2 TEASPOONS OF FLEUR DE SEL

---

*This type of butter is made the old-fashioned way—churned, rather than extracted with a centrifuge. If you can't find it in your stores, look for something else slow-churned.

Clean the radishes and trim off any unwanted greens. Cut into moderately thin slices. Dry and chill on a serving platter in the refrigerator to ensure they are cool and crispy.

Put the butter in a small bowl. Make sure there is enough for all of your guests (be generous)! Leave this on the counter until it is room temperature.

Slice the baguette into small 1- to 2-inch slices. If fresh, serve as is. If the baguette is a day old, lightly toast it.

Remove the radishes from the refrigerator and serve them alongside the bread, butter, and salt. Encourage guests to slather a piece of baguette with butter, sprinkle on salt, and top with a few radishes (and maybe a bit more salt).

Make sure you have plenty of Provençal rosé on hand to drink.

SERVES 5–10

STEAMED ARTICHOKES AND AIOLI

Sommeliers usually cringe when asked to pair artichokes with wine. This is because they contain a compound called "cynarin," which can sweeten the taste of wines. When in doubt, follow the rule that "what grows together, goes together." For centuries, people from the South of France have enjoyed artichokes and dry rosé. With this recipe, you'll see why.

ARTICHOKES

3—4 LARGE ARTICHOKES

2 BOTTLES OF BANDOL ROSÉ
(ONE TO COOK WITH, ONE TO DRINK)

1 HEAD OF GARLIC (2—3 CLOVES
FOR AIOLI)

1 LEMON, SLICED

2 BAY LEAVES

10 SPRIGS OF FLAT-LEAF PARSLEY

2 TABLESPOONS OF OLIVE OIL

1 TEASPOON SALT

AIOLI

2 GARLIC CLOVES, FROM A
ROASTED HEAD OF GARLIC

1 LARGE EGG YOLK

1 TABLESPOON LEMON JUICE,
FRESHLY SQUEEZED

1/4 TEASPOON SALT

1/4 CUP OLIVE OIL

ARTICHOKES: Preheat oven to 400°F. Place the wine, garlic, lemon, bay leaves, parsley, olive oil, and salt in a large pot. Bring to a simmer and cover.

Wash the artichokes under cold water. Cut off the stems of the artichokes close to the base. Pull off the lower petals that are small and tough. Cut off the top inch of the artichoke, just a tiny amount, rub this area with some lemon juice to keep the beautiful green color.

Place the artichokes in the steaming pot. Cover and simmer in the liquid for about 30 minutes in the oven or until tender.

Remove the artichoke and discard the liquid (or save for your next soup stock).

AIOLI: Cut off the tips of a head of garlic. Roast in the oven at 400°F, while simmering the liquid above, until the cloves are mushy, about 30 minutes. Use two of the cloves for the aioli. The rest can be saved in the refrigerator for a few days.

Combine the garlic, egg yolk, lemon juice, and salt in a food processor or blender to puree. (The absolute best aioli is made with a mortar and pestle, but this is a time-consuming method.) Add the oil in a slow stream and continue to process until the mixture has formed a thick emulsion. This might take a bit of time, so be patient!

SERVING: You can serve the artichoke hot or cold. Both are delicious. To eat, pull off a leaf, dip the tender little ends into the aioli, and scrape off the "meat" with your front teeth. Once you reach the center of the artichoke, remove the prickly cone and you will find the heart. This is the best and meatiest part. Make sure to share the heart and slather it in plenty of aioli. Drinking Bandol rosé alongside this dish is crucial to enjoying it fully.

SERVES 5–10

ANCHOVY TOASTS

Alice Waters allowed me to share this recipe she originally created for Kermit
Lynch in the 1970s to pair with Domaine Tempier Bandol rosé.

1 BAGUETTE

6 CLOVES OF GARLIC

1 8 OZ BOTTLE OF OLIVE OIL

1 PACKAGE OF ANCHOVIES
PACKED IN SALT

NIÇOISE OLIVES

BASIL LEAVES

DRIED TOMATOES

Cut a thin slice of good bread. Toast it. Rub it
with raw garlic. Saturate it with your best olive
oil. Repeat for the number of serving needed.

Filet an anchovy and rinse it well. Place the
anchovy shiny side up on the bread and broil
it until brown. Brush with olive oil. Serve with
Niçoise olives, basil leaves, dried tomatoes—
whatever you desire and have on hand.

SERVES 5–10

anchovies on toast

GIGONDAS POTATO AU GRATIN

Inspired by a recipe I once ate by Daniel Brunier of Vieux Télégraphe in Châteauneuf-du-Pape, this is the perfect decadent dish for heavier Provençal rosés from Tavel or Gigondas. If you can find the Daniel Brunier's Gigondas Pallières Rosé, it is the perfect excuse to make this delicious side dish.

---

2 CLOVES OF GARLIC

2 LARGE YELLOW ONIONS, THINLY SLICED

3 LBS BAKING POTATOES, THINLY SLICED

1/4 CUP CHICKEN FAT
(You can purchase at your butcher or save this from the "Roasted Chicken Provençal" recipe on page 106.)

2 1/2 CUPS CRÈME FRAÎCHE

1 CUP ROSÉ (FROM PROVENCE)

2 TABLESPOONS FLOUR

3 SPRIGS OF FRESH THYME

SALT AND PEPPER TO TASTE

Preheat oven to 350°F. Rub the garlic all over the inside of a baking dish, and then slice the garlic. Grease the dish with a bit of chicken fat.

Sauté onions in chicken fat until soft and brown. Combine them in a large saucepan with the potatoes, sliced garlic, crème fraîche, wine, flour, thyme, salt, and pepper. Bring to a boil over medium-high heat and cook, stirring constantly, until the mixture thickens slightly, 2–3 minutes.

Transfer to the baking dish, distributing evenly. Bake uncovered until the potatoes are soft, about 1 hour, occasionally spooning some of the liquid over the top. Let cool for a bit before serving.

SERVES 4–8

BLACK OLIVE TAPENADE

A recipe with few ingredients, but patience and a bit of strength is required if you choose to make it the old-fashioned way. Modern methods can hasten things up a bit, so keep this recipe in mind next time you have last-minute guests coming over.

½ LB LARGE BLACK OLIVES, PITTED

2 CLOVES OF GARLIC

2 ANCHOVIES PACKED IN SALT, RINSED AND FILLETED

1 TEASPOON FRESH THYME (OR SAVORY HERB SIMILAR TO THYME)

4 TABLESPOONS HIGH QUALITY OLIVE OIL

1 FRESH BAGUETTE

1 OR MORE BOTTLES OF CORSICAN ROSÉ

A mortar and pestle will truly elevate this dish. However, it is not essential and a food processor will do just fine. Place all of the ingredients (except for the oil) in the processor and mix until a fine paste. Add in the oil slowly until the mixture is a good chunky consistency.

If making it the traditional way with a mortar and pestle, muddle the garlic first until it is a fine paste. Then add the anchovies and herbs. Next, toss in the olives and crush them gently, mixing everything together until it is a nice and chunky consistency. Drizzle in the oil and mix with a spoon.

Serve with a sliced baguette and plenty of rosé.

SERVES 5–10

GOAT CHEESE WRAPPED IN GARLIC MUSTARD

This is a fun and easy recipe. You can wrap the goat cheese in whatever seasonal herbs or flowers you forage or find at the farmers market. My favorite variation is one you can only make in mid-spring, with garlic mustard leaves and violets.

1 LARGE PIECE OF FRESH GOAT CHEESE, ABOUT 8 OZ

7—10 LEAVES OF GARLIC MUSTARD (OR OTHER HERBACEOUS PLANTS)

A SMALL HANDFUL OF VIOLETS

1 TEASPOON FLEUR DE SEL

2 TABLESPOONS ROSÉ

2 TABLESPOONS OLIVE OIL

1 FRESH BAGUETTE

CHINON ROSÉ

Roll goat cheese into a ball and press cleaned leaves and flowers onto the sides. Once coated, roll it lightly in fleur de sel. Mix 2 tablespoons each of the rosé and the olive oil together. Drizzle it over the cheese.

Serve this tangy snack with a fresh baguette and make sure there is plenty of Chinon rosé to drink.

SERVES 5—10

LUNCHES
AND PICNICS

WHEN THE WEATHER IS NICE, PACK THESE LUNCHES
in a picnic basket and head to the nearest park or
lawn. Rosé can be enjoyed at any time, but the magic of
good food, sunshine, and a blanket is undeniable.

LANGUEDOC LETTUCES WITH ROSÉ VINAIGRETTE

Inspired by the simple salads served in the Languedoc, the trick to this recipe is having fresh and beautiful greens. Although best in spring and summer, this can be made year-round if you are close to a good market or grocery store.

---

2 OZ (4 TABLESPOONS) OLIVE OIL

2 OZ (4 TABLESPOONS) LANGUEDOC ROSÉ

1–2 CUPS OF GREENS, WHATEVER IS IN SEASON

A HANDFUL OF FRESH BREADCRUMBS

Mix together the oil and rosé in a bowl. Add in the greens and lightly toss until coated. Serve on large plates and sprinkle with breadcrumbs. Make sure not to let the rest of the Languedoc rosé go to waste. Enjoy a few glasses with the salad.

SERVES 3–5

PISSALADIÈRE

This onion pizza originated in Nice, where it was served early in the morning for breakfast. Now it is more common to find as part of a lunch spread. The anchovies can either be placed whole on the tart or in the form of a pissalat (anchovy paste).

TART DOUGH

1 CUP FLOUR

DASH OF SALT

10 TABLESPOONS BUTTER, CHILLED AND DICED

3 TABLESPOONS COLD WATER

TOPPING

4 TABLESPOONS OLIVE OIL

2 LBS SWEET ONIONS, THINLY SLICED

8 ANCHOVIES PACKED IN SALT, RINSED AND FILLETED

1/2 CUP NIÇOISE OLIVES, PITTED

2 OZ (4 TABLESPOONS) FRESH THYME

2 BAY LEAVES

SALT AND PEPPER TO TASTE

TART DOUGH: Mix flour and salt in a bowl. Add butter and crumble together, being careful not to overwork dough or soften butter. Add cold water to the mixture and mix with a fork. Form into a ball, wrap in plastic wrap, and refrigerate for 1–2 hours. Using a floured surface, roll the dough into a rectangular shape about 12 inches long and ⅛-inch thick. Fold up the edges with your fingers or a fork.

TOPPING: Warm 2 tablespoons olive oil in a large sauté pan. Add in the onions, a dash of salt, bay leaves, and thyme. Cook covered, over low heat, stirring occasionally for about an hour. Once the onions are caramelized and so tender that they almost resemble a puree, remove the lid so the juices evaporate, about 10–15 minutes. Make sure that the heat stays low and the onions do not turn color. Season with salt and pepper.

Preheat oven to 375°F. Place topping on the dough and arrange a simple design with the anchovies (latticework looks nice). Place the olives in between the filets. Drizzle olive oil over the top and bake for about 20–30 minutes or until the edges are crispy.

You can serve this dish right away or at room temperature. You can leave it on the counter, covered for a few days, enjoying a piece here and there throughout the week. Whatever you decide, make sure there is plenty of Cassis rosé to be had alongside it.

Minerality and salinity (from the iodine of the sea) is what is best represented in our wine, with a delicate texture. That's why it is very interesting to combine them with Mediterranean seafood dishes like Pissaladière.

—JONATHAN SACK-ZAFIROPULO
Clos Sainte Magdeleine, Cassis

SERVES 5–10

OCTOPUS AND WHITE BEAN SALAD

When it starts to get warmer outside you can enjoy this classic dish chilled, served at the same temperature as your rosé. This dish is best when made a day ahead of time.

OCTOPUS

8 TABLESPOONS OLIVE OIL, DIVIDED

3 ½ LBS OCTOPUS
(Preferably fresh or frozen and thawed), mostly tentacles

1 LARGE YELLOW ONION, CHOPPED

3 GARLIC CLOVES, PEELED AND CRUSHED

3 FRESH SPRIGS FLAT-LEAF PARSLEY

2 BOTTLES OF ITALIAN ROSÉ (ROSATO)

1 TABLESPOON WHOLE BLACK PEPPERCORNS

1 TEASPOON SALT

2 BAY LEAVES

2 TABLESPOONS FRESH LEMON JUICE

1 TABLESPOON FRESH OREGANO, SAGE, AND ROSEMARY, CHOPPED

BEANS

1 CUP WHITE BEANS (COOKED)

2 TABLESPOONS OLIVE OIL

FRESHLY GROUND SALT AND PEPPER TO TASTE

A HANDFUL OF FRESH ARUGULA LEAVES, WASHED AND DRIED

AGED BALSAMIC VINEGAR, TO DRESS

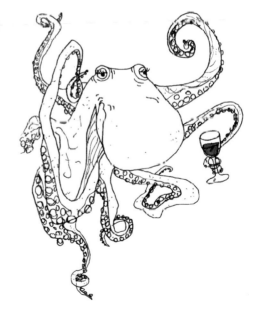

In a large pot, add 2 tablespoons of oil and bring to a moderately high heat. Add the octopus and cook, uncovered, for about 20 minutes, or until most of the liquid in the pot evaporates. Add onions, garlic, parsley, wine, pepper, salt, and the bay leaves. Reduce to a simmer, cover, and cook for about 2 hours.

Once the octopus is tender, pull it out of the pot and let the tentacles rest for 10–15 minutes. Then, cut the tentacles crosswise in slices ¼-inch thick. Brush with 2 tablespoons of olive oil and sprinkle with freshly ground salt and pepper. Grill these slices either on the grill outside or in a pan, for about 2 minutes per side. Transfer to a large bowl. Add the remaining oil, lemon juice, oregano, sage, and rosemary. If serving the next day, place the octopus in an airtight container and store in the refrigerator.

In a separate bowl, add the beans, olive oil, salt, pepper, and arugula. Toss until well mixed. If you are making this for the next day, do not mix in the arugula; keep this on the side until just before serving. Chill for a day in an airtight container in the refrigerator for the next day or serve warm immediately.

To serve, place the bean salad on plates and top with the grilled octopus. Drizzle a touch of very aged balsamic vinegar for an extra kick.

Make sure you have extra rosato to drink.

SERVES 3–5

SMOKED SALMON SPREAD

This delicious spread is the perfect dish for brunch or lunch. It can be made a day or two ahead of time and stored in the refrigerator.

---

8 OZ PIECE OF UNCOOKED SALMON, BONES REMOVED

4 OZ SMOKED SALMON, CUT INTO THIN STRIPS
(This can be purchased cooked)

1 TABLESPOON OLIVE OIL

6 TABLESPOONS BEURRE DE BARATTE, ROOM TEMPERATURE

1 1/2 TEASPOONS LEMON JUICE, FRESHLY SQUEEZED

3 TABLESPOONS CHIVES, CHOPPED

1/4 TEASPOON FRESHLY GROUND WHITE OR PINK PEPPERCORNS

SALT TO TASTE

1 FRESH BAGUETTE, SLICED, TOASTED, AND WITH A BIT OF BUTTER

Salt the uncooked salmon and steam for about 7 minutes. Remove the salmon from the heat and let it cool. Remove the skin.

In a small bowl, mix together the oil and butter. Add in the chives, lemon juice, and smoked salmon, folding everything gently until well integrated. Add in the ground peppercorns and additional salt to taste. Mix in the steamed salmon.

I like to serve this dish by packing the spread into small, round, glass containers and covering the tops with plastic wrap. Let them cool on the counter for a bit to firm up. Then flip the containers over (making sure the plastic wrap is firmly holding everything in) and store them, upside down, in the refrigerator. Refrigerate overnite. The next day, you will notice that there is a small film of fat that has formed on the surface. Peel off the plastic wrap, and add a small scoop of spread to each piece of bread, gently breaking through the layer of fat each time.

For such a rich dish, make sure you have plenty of racy and refreshing rosé Champagne to pair.

SERVES 3–5

FARRO SALAD

A healthy dish that can be made with anything you pick up from the farmers market.

SALAD

1 CUP FARRO

¾ CUP WATER

¼ CUP ROSÉ VERMOUTH

1 LARGE GRAPEFRUIT PEEL

2 BAY LEAVES

SALT AND PEPPER TO TASTE

8 TABLESPOONS OLIVE OIL

2 TABLESPOONS LEMON JUICE, FRESHLY SQUEEZED

½ CUP SHAVED PARMESAN CHEESE

½ CUP PISTACHIOS, CHOPPED

VEGETABLES

Substitute vegetables based on what is in season. My favorite combination:

2 CUPS GREENS (KALE, SWISS CHARD, AND ARUGULA) WASHED AND THINLY SLICED

1 CUP FRESH BASIL LEAVES, GENTLY TORN

¼ CUP FRESH MINT

¾ CUP CHOPPED GRAPE TOMATOES

⅓ CUP RADISHES, THINLY SLICED

Cook the farro over medium heat with the water, rosé, grapefruit peels, bay leaves, salt, and pepper. Cook until the grains are tender. Remove extra liquid, if needed, and set aside to cool. Once the farro is cooled, mix in olive oil, lemon juice, cheese, and pistachios. This will keep for up to a week in the refrigerator. Toss in fresh vegetables when ready to serve.

Serve with a nice bottle of Tavel rosé.

SERVES 3–5

PROVENÇAL VEGETABLE SOUP (SOUPE AU PISTOU)

This Provençal vegetable soup is perfect for a hearty lunch on a cool day. Pistou is essentially a pesto sauce which is drizzled into the broth at the end. The best way to serve it Is with baguettes slathered in plenty of goat cheese for dipping. It tastes best a day (or two) after it is made.

SOUP

1 1/2 CUPS WHITE BEANS (CANNED OR PRE-SOAKED)

1 LARGE SLICE PANCETTA

1 QUART WATER

1 QUART BANDOL ROSÉ

1 LARGE YELLOW ONION, CHOPPED

5 GARLIC CLOVES, MINCED

1 BOUQUET GARNI*

1 TABLESPOON HIGH QUALITY OLIVE OIL

2 LEEKS, CLEANED AND CHOPPED, WHITE PARTS ONLY

1 LB PEELED TOMATOES (CANNED OR FRESH)

2 CUPS SAVOY CABBAGE, FINELY CUT

2 LARGE CARROTS, DICED

2 CELERY STALKS, DICED

1 LARGE ZUCCHINI, DICED

2 TURNIPS, PEELED AND DICED

1/2 CUP PASTA SHELLS

SALT AND PEPPER TO TASTE

---

*Bouquet garni are fresh herbs (rosemary, sage, oregano, parsley, bay leaf, thyme) tied together and used in cooking soups. Remove prior to serving.

PISTOU

2 GARLIC CLOVES, HALVED

2 CUPS OF FRESH BASIL LEAVES, TIGHTLY PACKED

1/3 CUP HIGH QUALITY OLIVE OIL

1/2 CUP OF FRESHLY GRATED PARMESAN CHEESE

SALT AND PEPPER TO TASTE

1 FRESH BAGUETTE

6—8 TABLESPOONS FRESH GOAT CHEESE TO SPREAD

In a large pot, add the beans, pancetta, water, and wine and bring to a boil. Skim off any foam. Add half of the onion, half of the garlic, and the entire bouquet garni. Reduce the heat and simmer for 45 minutes. Add salt and pepper to taste. Turn off heat.

In a pan, heat olive oil and add in the remaining onion with salt. Cook until tender (about 5 minutes). Add in leeks and remaining garlic. Cook for 2–3 minutes, then add the tomatoes. Make sure you stir every 15 seconds or so. Once the tomatoes have cooked down a bit, about 10 minutes, add the ingredients to the big soup pot. Add the other vegetables to the soup pot. Bring it back to a simmer and cook for about an hour.

While this is cooking, make the pistou. Just like you would make pesto, mash the garlic with a mortar and pestle (or use a food processor). Add in the basil leaves, then the oil and cheese. Add salt and pepper to taste.

About 10–15 minutes before serving, add the pasta to the soup.

When serving, ladle a good helping into each bowl. Drizzle a sizable amount of the pistou into the soup and rest a baguette with goat cheese on the side of the bowl. Make sure a few bottles of Bandol rosé are readily available to drink.

SERVES 5–10

ENTRÉES
AND FEASTS

ROSÉ REALLY COMES ALIVE WHEN SHARED IN GROUPS.
Whether you are doing a late night bonfire party, a Sunday cookout,
or a winter dinner party, these are the recipes to try.
Each recipe serves around 4–8 people.

LULU'S BOUILLABAISSE

Adapted from a recipe created by Domaine Tempier's very own Lulu Peyraud, this is the quintessential Provençal dish to accompany rosé.

MARINADE

POWDERED FENNEL SEED

1/8 TEASPOON POWDERED SAFFRON

5 GARLIC CLOVES, PEELED AND CRUSHED

4 TABLESPOONS OLIVE OIL

SOUP STOCK

4 TABLESPOONS OLIVE OIL

1 LARGE ONION, SLICED

1 HEAD GARLIC, EACH CLOVE SEPARATED AND CRUSHED

2 TOMATOES, QUARTERED

2–3 LBS FISH BONES BROKEN INTO SMALL PIECES
(Ask your local fishmonger for these. Most are more than happy to give away the heads and carcasses free. Make sure the gills are removed.)

8 SMALL BLUE CRABS

2 QUARTS WATER

1 QUART BANDOL ROSÉ

1 TEASPOON POWDERED FENNEL SEEDS

1 LEEK, FINELY SLICED

1 CELERY STALK, SLICED

2 CARROTS, PEELED AND SLICED

SALT AND PEPPER TO TASTE

SOUP FILLINGS

6 LBS WHITE-FLESH WHOLE SALTWATER FISH, CUT INTO SERVING PORTIONS
(Lulu always includes rascasse, weevers, and anglerfish but you can see what the local fish market has to offer.)

1/4 TEASPOON SAFFRON

8 MEDIUM POTATOES, PEELED AND QUARTERED

1 LARGE SWEET WHITE ONION, SLICED VERY THIN

2 TOMATOES, PEELED, SEEDED, AND COARSELY CHOPPED (FRESH OR CANNED)

5 GARLIC CLOVES, PEELED AND CRUSHED

A PINCH OF POWDERED FENNEL SEEDS

1 1/2 LBS MUSSELS, SOAKED IN WATER WITH SALT, SCRAPED, DEBEARDED, AND RINSED

ROUILLÉ

(This is a sauce that is an essential garnish to bouillabaisse. This can also be purchased pre-made at specialty grocery stores.)

1 CUP FRESH BREADCRUMBS (NO CRUST)

1/4 TEASPOON POWDERED SAFFRON DISSOLVED IN 2 TABLESPOONS OF HOT SOUP

A LARGE PINCH OF CAYENNE PEPPER POWDER

A LARGE PINCH OF COARSE SALT

3 GARLIC CLOVES, PEELED

1 EGG YOLK

2 CUPS OLIVE OIL

TOAST

FRENCH SOURDOUGH

1 GARLIC CLOVE, PEELED

To be meaningful, certain dishes in Provence must
gather together all the family or very dear friends
around a single dish—but what a dish!

—FROM *Lulu's Provençale Table*
by Richard Olney

SOUP STOCK: Combine all marinade ingredients. Marinate
6 pounds of white-flesh saltwater fish in the prepared marinade for at least 2 hours.

While this is marinating, start preparing the soup stock.
Warm the olive oil over medium-low heat and add the
onion and garlic. Stir regularly until the onions are soft.
Add the tomatoes and fish bones, mashing them up slowly
with the back of your spoon until they are broken down.
Add the crabs and cook until they turn red in color. Add
enough water and Bandol rosé to cover everything. Stir
continuously. Bring to a boil and skim any foam that forms
on the surface.

Add salt, pepper, fennel seeds, leeks, celery, and carrots.
Keep the lid ajar and simmer for 45 minutes. After 5–10
minutes, remove the crabs and put to the side. With a mortar and pestle, break up the shells thoroughly and spoon
them back into the soup.

Once the stock is done, run it through a sieve multiple
times. It is important to make sure there are no small fish
bones left.

ROUILLE: Place the breadcrumbs in a bowl and mash them
with the saffron that has been dissolved in a bit of hot soup

stock. Add a bit more fish stock to form a loose paste. Using a mortar and pestle, combine the cayenne pepper, salt, and garlic. Ground to a paste. Add the egg yolk and the saffron bread paste. Mix until smooth. Very slowly trickle in the oil while constantly stirring, like you were making mayonnaise. Let this sit for a bit while the soup is finishing.

SOUP FILLINGS: Add the saffron, potatoes, onions, tomatoes, garlic, and fennel seeds to the stock. Bring to a boil. After 5 minutes, add the mussels. Five minutes after that, add the marinated fish and boil for 10 minutes.

With a slotted spoon, lift the fish onto a large and warm platter. Scoop out the mussels and potatoes and place these on another platter.

TOAST: Thinly slice a loaf of French sourdough and lightly toast. Rub each side with a peeled and cut garlic clove.

SERVING: This is where the fun comes in. Smear the toasted garlic bread with plenty of rouille and place a piece into each bowl. Ladle the hot soup over the bread and hand out to hungry guests. Pass around the platters of fish, mussels, and potatoes so guests can add as they please. Magnums of Bandol rosé are required. You will quickly find one or two bottles will not be enough for a group.

SERVES 10–15

LAVENDER AND HAY ROASTED LAMB

Served with summer Provençal vegetables. This recipe comes from Jim Gop at Heirloom Fire, a company based in the Berkshires of Massachusetts that caters magical events, cooking everything over a wood fire.

LAMB

1 5-LB LEG OF LAMB OR 2 ½ LB LAMB SHOULDER

10 GARLIC CLOVES, PEELED AND SLICED IN HALF LENGTHWISE

3 TABLESPOONS OLIVE OIL

SALT AND PEPPER

1 ½ BAG EATING HAY (CAN BE PURCHASED AT A PET SHOP)

1 CUP DRIED LAVENDER LEAVES

4 SPRIGS OF ROSEMARY, DIVIDED

SUMMER PROVENÇAL VEGETABLES

2 TABLESPOONS OLIVE OIL

1 ZUCCHINI, DICED INTO 1-INCH CUBES

1 SUMMER SQUASH, DICED INTO 1-INCH CUBES

2 LBS ASSORTED TOMATOES (CHERRIES AND FULL SIZE); CHERRIES HALVED, FULL-SIZED DICED

1 CLOVE GARLIC, PEELED AND MINCED

½ LB FRENCH GREEN BEANS, STEMMED, BLANCHED, AND CUT ON A BIAS

1 TABLESPOON UNSALTED BUTTER

½ A LEMON, JUICED

HANDFUL OF FRESH BASIL LEAVES, ROUGHLY CHOPPED

Preheat oven to 350°F.

Place a cast iron Dutch oven or a deep heatproof roasting pan over medium-low flame.

Make 20 small incisions all around the lamb and push the garlic slices into each of the slits. Drizzle the lamb with the olive oil and season with salt and pepper. Set aside.

When the Dutch oven is hot to the touch, remove from the heat. Working quickly to retain the heat in the pan, arrange the hay in the base, sprinkle with ½ cup lavender leaves and 2 sprigs of rosemary. Tuck the lamb into the center of the hay nest and sprinkle the remaining ½ cup lavender leaves over it. Gently cover the lamb with a thin layer of hay, put the lid on or cover with aluminum foil. Put into the oven. If the Dutch oven has lost too much heat, put it back on the fire for 3 minutes with the lamb inside before putting it into the oven. Allow the lamb to cook for 2 hours. After 2 hours, remove the lid or foil and increase the temperature to 400°F. Cook for an additional 30 minutes. Remove from the oven and let rest for 10 minutes.

Place a large sauté pan over medium flame and add 2 tablespoons olive oil. Strip the remaining 2 sprigs of rosemary and chop roughly. Reserve. Add the zucchini and summer squash to the pan and sauté for 2 minutes. Next, add the tomatoes, garlic, and beans and cook for 1 minute or until the beans are warmed through, stirring occasionally. Add butter and lemon juice, gently shaking and stirring the pan to create a sauce. Remove the pan from the heat and stir in rosemary and basil. Adjust seasoning with salt and pepper.

Lay out plates. Generously spoon vegetable mixture onto the center of each plate. Remove the lamb from the cast iron and remove any excess hay from the roast. Place meat on a carving board and cut meat against the grain. Lay on top of vegetables.

OPTIONAL: Place a colander into a large bowl and empty hay and contents of roasting pan into the colander. Collect any juice that has accumulated from the bowl and spoon over meat.

Plenty of rosé should be served with this dish. A rosé with some structure and body is recommended; think Provence, Corsica, and Cerasuolo d'Abruzzo.

SERVES 5–10

ROSÉ SOUP

This is a quick and easy dish that will never disappoint. It is an Austrian speciality and is perfect for those cold winter nights when you need something a little heartier.

1 YELLOW ONION, DICED

2 TABLESPOONS BUTTER

1 BOTTLE OF SCHILCHER ROSÉ
(1 CUP TO COOK WITH, THE REST TO
DRINK)

2 CUPS VEGETABLE STOCK

2 GARLIC CLOVES, SLICED

1 NUTMEG CLOVE SHAVED TO AT
LEAST 2 TEASPOONS

6 SPRIGS FRESH THYME

2 MEDIUM POTATOES

1 CUP HEAVY CREAM

SALT AND PEPPER TO TASTE

GARNISH

TOASTED PUMPKIN SEEDS

CREAM TO DRIZZLE

PUMPKIN SEED OIL TO DRIZZLE

Sauté onion in the butter. Add 1 cup of wine. Reduce this mixture and remove from the heat. Mix this together with the vegetable stock in a larger pot. Add garlic, nutmeg, and thyme. Slice the potatoes and add to the pot. Bring everything to a boil.

Once the potatoes are soft, add in the cream. Put all ingredients in a blender to puree until smooth. Add salt and pepper to taste.

To serve, ladle into bowls and garnish with pumpkin seeds, pumpkin seed oil, and cream.

SERVES 5–10

MUSSELS AND FRENCH FRIES

Any good French restaurant will serve heaping bowls of mussels. This rendition swaps the white wine for rosé, accompanied with plenty of french fries, of course.

MAYONNAISE

1 TEASPOON DIJON MUSTARD

1 EGG YOLK

1 CUP OLIVE OIL

2 TEASPOONS WHITE WINE VINEGAR

2 TEASPOONS LEMON JUICE, FRESHLY SQUEEZED

SALT AND PEPPER TO TASTE

FRIES

2 LBS RUSSET POTATOES, CUT INTO FRY STICKS

FRYING OIL (VEGETABLE OR PEANUT)

SALT

MUSSELS

2 1/2 LBS MUSSELS (SCRUBBED AND DEBEARDED)

2/3 CUP PROVENÇAL ROSÉ

2 TABLESPOONS BUTTER, CUBED

2 GARLIC CLOVES, FINELY SLICED

1 LEEK, THINLY SLICED

1/2 YELLOW ONION, FINELY CHOPPED

SALT AND PEPPER TO TASTE

MAYONNAISE: Whisk together the mustard and egg yolk, slowly adding in the oil until it emulsifies. Then add vinegar, lemon juice, salt, and pepper. This mayonnaise is essential to the recipe.

MUSSELS AND FRENCH FRIES: Start the french fries before the mussels, since the latter doesn't take very long. Add oil to a deep pot and heat oil to about 375°F. Place a fry in the oil to check the sizzle and temperature before adding a handful at a time. Cook for 8–10 minutes, to the desired level of crispness. Transfer to paper towels to let cool and drain. Season with salt to taste.

In a big pot, add the wine, butter, garlic, leeks, onions, salt, and pepper. Cover with a lid. After a few minutes and once the mixture is well combined, add the mussels. Shake the pot occasionally and cook for about 5 minutes. Once all the mussels have opened, use a slotted spoon to remove them from the pot. Divide into bowls and pour the broth over the mussels to cover them. Serve with the fries, mayonnaise, and leftover rosé.

SERVES 5–10

RICOTTA GNOCCHI WITH BROCCOLI PESTO, ENGLISH PEAS, AND LOCAL MUSHROOMS IN OLIVE OIL

This recipe was given to me by my coworker and Michelin star chef Chris Cipollone. Although the name sounds fancy, it is actually quite easy to make. Impress all of your friends with this delicious pasta dish that goes exceptionally well with rosé.

GNOCCHI

1 CUP RICOTTA

1 EGG

1 CUP ALL-PURPOSE FLOUR

PESTO

1 HEAD BROCCOLI, FLORETS AND TOP STEMS BLANCHED AND ROUGHLY CHOPPED

1 CUP PINE NUTS, TOASTED

1 CUP BASIL LEAVES

1 GARLIC CLOVE

1/2 CUP PARMESAN CHEESE, GRATED

1 CUP OLIVE OIL

SALT AND PEPPER TO TASTE

MUSHROOMS IN OLIVE OIL

2 CUPS VARIOUS MUSHROOMS, CLEANED AND OVEN-ROASTED UNTIL FULLY COOKED

4 TABLESPOONS OLIVE OIL

3 TABLESPOONS SHERRY VINEGAR

1 TABLESPOON SHALLOTS, MINCED

1 TEASPOON GARLIC, MINCED

1/2 TEASPOON CHILI FLAKES

SALT TO TASTE

FOR SERVING

1 CUP ENGLISH PEAS, FRESH OR FROZEN AND BLANCHED

GNOCCHI: Mix together the ricotta and egg. Add in the flour until it is just incorporated. Do not overwork the dough. Let it rest in the refrigerator for 1 hour. On a lightly floured surface, roll the dough into a 1-inch diameter tube and cut into 1-inch pieces. Add to boiling water for 15–30 seconds, or until the gnocchi start to rise to the surface. Remove from the water and put to the side.

PESTO: Blanch the broccoli and then dry thoroughly. Place in a food processor and pulse the broccoli with pine nuts, basil leaves, and garlic until the texture is almost smooth, but slightly chunky. Add the Parmesan cheese and drizzle in the olive oil while the machine is running. Season with salt and pepper to taste.

MUSHROOMS IN OLIVE OIL: Add the last six ingredients to the roasted mushrooms and marinate for up to an hour.

SERVING: Scoop some gnocchi and English peas into bowls and toss with the pesto. Add a bit of the mushrooms in olive oil on top of each portion.

SERVES 4–5

TROUT EN PAPILLOTE

En papillote is French for "in parchment." This is a superb method since it requires no cleanup, doesn't make your whole house smell fishy, and cooks the fish perfectly.

4 PARCHMENT PAPER BAGS, PARCHMENT PAPER, OR ALUMINUM FOIL

4 TABLESPOONS BUTTER, DICED

4 TROUT FILETS (ABOUT THE SIZE OF YOUR PALM)

1/2 SMALL YELLOW ONION, SLICED

2 CLOVES GARLIC, MINCED

OLIVE OIL TO DRIZZLE

1/4 CUP PROVENÇAL ROSÉ

2 LEMON WHEELS

A FEW SPRIGS OF FRESH THYME AND ROSEMARY

SALT TO TASTE

The premise of this dish is to serve the fish in parchment paper parcels, letting it rest in a delicious broth of wine, butter, and herbs. That being said, if you do not have parchment paper or bags, you can use aluminum foil and serve the fish, removed, in a bowl.

Preheat the oven to 375°F.

If using aluminum foil or parchment paper, rip off a good size piece and put a few pieces of butter in the center of one half. Place a filet on top of this. Add the other ingredients on top. Fold the edges of the foil or paper together, forming a seal so no liquid can escape. Don't fold the package too tightly. You want to make sure the fish is steaming inside, so allow enough space to do so. Do this for each filet so you have four little parcels or packages.

Place the fish in the oven and cook for 10–12 minutes. I like my fish a bit undercooked, but some might prefer it to be a little firmer. Serve immediately with the leftover rosé.

SERVES 4 PEOPLE

ROASTED CHICKEN PROVENÇAL

Over the last few years, on Saturday mornings my little sister Laura and I would go to the farmers market and pick up a fresh chicken for Sunday dinner. It was the one time a week when she didn't have school and I didn't have to work in the restaurant. For a while, Sundays and roasted chicken were synonymous. The ritual of cooking together, having the whole house smell like the South of France, and enjoying a bottle of wine was magical. These days, we have gotten busier, but every now and then we still have a roasted chicken on Sunday. The magic of this dish is that it involves little time around the stove and brings people together in enjoyment.

BRINE

1 BOTTLE PROVENÇAL ROSÉ

13 CUPS WATER

1 CUP KOSHER SALT

CHICKEN

1 4–5 LB WHOLE CHICKEN

4 GARLIC CLOVES

LOTS OF SOUTHERN FRENCH HERBS (ROSEMARY, THYME, MARJORAM)

1 LEMON, CUT INTO WHEELS

OLIVE OIL

SALT AND PEPPER

BRINE: In a large pot, dissove salt with the liquids in the brine. Submerge the chicken. Leave this in the refrigerator overnight.

BAKING: Remove the bird from the brine and rinse quickly. Place on a rack and let dry for 10 minutes. Preheat the oven to 400°F. Combine garlic, herbs, salt, and pepper in a bowl, then add olive oil until it makes a thick mixture. Rub this all over the chicken. Stuff the inside of the chicken with extra herbs and lemon wheels. Tie the legs together with kitchen twine, place in a large roasting pan, and put it into the oven.

Roast the chicken until the skin starts to brown, around 25–30 minutes. Reduce the heat to 350°F and cook for another 30 minutes. Let rest for at least 20 minutes before carving.

Serve with Provençal rosé and Languedoc Lettuces with Rosé Vinaigrette (see the recipe under "Lunches and Picnics") and Gigondas Potato au Gratin (see the recipe under "Snacks and Sides").

SERVES 4–6

DESSERTS

AFTER A FEW BOTTLES OF WINE AND A BIG MEAL,
I often prefer to end on a simple, sweet note with desserts
that are easy to make. Here are a few to try.

FIGS ROASTED WITH GOAT CHEESE

This recipe was given to me by Angéline Templier of Champagne J. Lassalle. The ingredients that originally went into this dish were from her friends at Vieux Télégraphe in Châteauneuf-du-Pape, France. Outside of making delicious wine, Daniel Brunier raises goats for cheese and makes olive oil from his groves.

8 FIGS

1 TEASPOON LAVENDER HONEY
(Infuse the honey by adding fresh lavender, heating it up, letting it cool, then resting for a few days.)

2 WHEELS OF FRESH GOAT CHEESE

8 FRESH ROSEMARY SPRIGS

OLIVE OIL TO DRIZZLE

SEA SALT

AGED BALSAMIC VINEGAR TO DRIZZLE

MESCLUN

1/4 CUP PINE NUTS

1/4 CUP CHIVES

TOAST

Wash the figs and slice in half, lengthwise without cutting all the way through. Pour lavender honey on each half. Slice the goat cheese and lay a bit on each fig. Place a rosemary sprig on top of the cheese. Drizzle the prepared figs with a bit of olive oil. Place the figs in the oven at 375°F for 10 minutes.

Meanwhile, toss a bit of mesclun with balsamic vinegar and olive oil. Add pine nuts and chives. Put a bit of this salad on each plate, along with a slice of toast spread with some extra goat cheese, topped with sea salt. Once the figs are roasted, place on the salad and serve while still warm.

Drink with Champagne or other sparkling wine, maybe something a bit sweet like Bugey-Cerdon or a pét-nat.

SERVES 4–6

SUMMER PUDDING

This no-fuss dish makes for a bold finish. Brightly colored, it is a cheerful dessert that even a novice cook can make. It is not as much a pudding but rather bread soaked in berries and wine.

---

6 CUPS MIXED SUMMER BERRIES (FRESH OR FROZEN AND THAWED)

1/2 CUP SUGAR

1/3 CUP WATER

1 TABLESPOON LEMON JUICE, FRESHLY SQUEEZED

A FEW TEASPOONS OF ROSÉ, LIKE BUGEY-CERDON

10–12 SLICES SOFT WHITE BREAD, CRUSTS REMOVED

WHIPPED CREAM OR VANILLA ICE CREAM TO SERVE

Combine berries, sugar, and water in a pan. Simmer on low heat until sugar is dissolved and the berries have released their juices, about 7–10 minutes. Stir in the lemon juice and the rosé. Pour a bit of the juice, without the berries, into a loaf pan. Line with a single layer of bread, cut into pieces to fit. Place about a third of the fruit on top of the bread. Once completely coated, top with another layer of bread. Continue alternating layers of fruit and bread. Make sure to end with bread as the top layer.

Let this sit on the counter and cool completely. Then wrap the whole pan tightly in plastic wrap and place a light weight (like a thick glass plate) on top of the pudding, to compress it a bit. Refrigerate at least 6 hours or overnight.

To serve, run a knife around the sides of the pan, then turn it over onto a plate to unmold. Serve in slices with whipped cream or ice cream on top. Enjoy with a glass or two of Bugey-Cerdon.

SERVES 4–6

ROSÉ JAM AND ALMOND BUTTER ON BRIOCHE

This tart rosé jam is easy to make and can be used in many different dishes. Here, it contrasts the richness of the nut butter and nestles perfectly onto a fluffy slab of brioche.

8 CUPS RED BERRIES (RASPBERRIES OR STRAWBERRIES)

2 CUPS SUGAR

1/4 CUP OF PROVENÇAL ROSÉ

ALMOND BUTTER

BRIOCHE

This is a fun recipe that lets you get your hands dirty. Combine everything but the brioche in a large bowl and mush together with your hands. Once the berries are broken down, transfer to a saucepan and bring to a boil over high heat. Stir often. Reduce the heat and keep stirring until it has thickened, about 10–15 minutes.

Cut slices of brioche and plate. Top each slice with a bit of almond butter. Add the warm jam and serve with chilled rosé.

SERVES 4–6

ROSÉ LEMON SORBET

A cool treat and a refreshing way to finish a meal. Super simple, yet refined.

2 CUPS OF DRY ROSÉ (LIKE TAVEL)

½ CUP SUGAR

1 LEMON, PEELED INTO WIDE STRIPS WITH A VEGETABLE PEELER

½ CUP LEMON JUICE

1 CUP WATER

In a small pan, combine rosé, sugar, and the lemon peels. Cook over moderate heat until the sugar dissolves, about 5 minutes. Remove from heat, then add lemon juice and water. Remove the lemon peels. Pour this final mixture into ice cube trays or shallow containers. Freeze overnight.

Take the frozen mixture out of the freezer and place in a food processor. Use the "pulse" setting to break it up until smooth, but still icy. Scoop the sorbet into a shallow container and freeze again until completely set. This will take another 6–8 hours.

Garnish with any berries or citrus fruits and serve with leftover rosé.

SERVES 4–6

ACKNOWLEDGMENTS

I WOULD LIKE TO THANK MY LITERARY AGENT, ALLISON HUNTER, FOR FINDING me in a maddening world of sommeliers and trusting me to write a decent book. Also, many thanks to HarperCollins and my editor, Rebecca Hunt, who put up with my slew of emails.

Thanks to my family for their support, my sister Sarah James and cousin Lauren Tillotson for helping me with logistics, and my sister Laura James for proofreading, and doing the dishes that piled up while I wrote this book.

Many thanks to everyone at Piora for their contributions and help while I was exhaustively writing and working the floor every night. Special thanks to Jeffrey O'Connor, Jin Park, and Simon and Nayun Kim for their constant support.

Thank you to the American Sommelier Association, Court of Master Sommeliers, Lattanzi's, Harry's, Aureole, Ristorante Morini, Marea, Piora, and to the countless organizations and people that made me the sommelier I am today.

Thanks to all of my brave blind-tasting guinea pigs: Luke Boland, Kyle Ridington, Elan Moss, Jeff Porter, Dean Fuerth, Vicki Denig, Jane Lopes, Ryan Totman, Carrie Lyn Strong, Wesley Sohn, Jeffrey O'Connor, Erin Gotthelf, and anonymous tasters.

A very special thanks to Jana Warchalowski who has always been there for me.

Immense gratitude to Roger Park for following and supporting my career.

Lastly, thank you to my boyfriend and illustrator, Lyle Railsback. Your patience and kindness made this book possible. Thank you for bringing my words to life with your beautiful drawings and for loving me unconditionally.

ABOUT THE AUTHOR

GEOFF KRUTH

Victoria James has worked in restaurants since she was thirteen. She fell in love with wine and when she was twenty-one became certified as a sommelier. She has worked at some of the most prestigious restaurants in New York City including Marea and Aureole. She is now the corporate beverage director of Piora in the West Village, and their new restaurant Cote. Victoria's name has appeared on many notable lists: Zagat's *30 Under 30*, Wine Enthusiast's *40 Under 40*, Forbes' *10 Innovators Under 30 Shaking Up the New York Food Scene*, Wine & Spirits *Best New Sommeliers*, and thebacklabel.com declared her "New York's Youngest Sommelier." She travels as much as possible to vineyards around the world and writes about the stories behind the wines. In her free time, she makes Amaro from foraged plants. She lives in New York City with her sister Laura, her boyfriend, Lyle, and her dog, Rocco.

Follow her on Instagram/Twitter: @Geturgrapeon or check out the latest news at www.geturgrapeon.com.

ABOUT THE ILLUSTRATOR

ERIN GOTTHELF

Lyle Railsback was born in California, has an art degree from George Fox University in Oregon, and makes wine with his brother in Santa Ynez, California. Their first release as Railsback Frères was a rosé inspired by Lulu Peyraud in Bandol. Currently, he does national sales for Kermit Lynch Wine Merchant and travels a lot.

Follow him on Instaram: @lylerailsback or check out the latest news at www.lylerailsback.com.

RETAIL SHOPS WITH GREAT ROSÉ SELECTIONS

ARIZONA

French Grocery, Phoenix

La Grande Orange Grocery, Phoenix

The Wine Store at Tarbell's, Phoenix

Time Market, Tucson

CALIFORNIA

Arlequin Wine Merchant, San Francisco

Dig Wines, San Francisco

Domaine LA, Los Angeles

Ferry Plaza Wine Merchant, San Francisco

Hi-Time Wine Cellars, Costa Mesa

Kermit Lynch Wine Merchant, Berkeley

Les Marchands Wine Bar & Merchant, Santa Barbara

Lincoln Beverage, Los Angeles (Venice)

San Francisco Wine Trading Company, San Francisco

Sherry-Lehmann Wine and Spirits, Los Angeles

Silverlake Wine, Los Angeles

The Wine Exchange, Santa Ana

The Wine House, Los Angeles

Vin, Vino, Wine, Palo Alto

COLORADO

Boulder Wine Merchant, Boulder

Cured, Boulder

Mondo Vino, Denver

The Proper Pour, Denver

CONNECTICUT

Ancona's Wines & Liquors, Ridgefield

HAWAII

Fujioka's Wine Times, Honolulu

Kamuela Liquor Store, Waimea

R Field Wine Company at Foodland, Kailua

Tamura's Fine Wine & Liquors, multiple locations

IDAHO

Boise Co-op Wine Shop, Boise

ILLINOIS

Binny's Beverage Depot, Chicago

Independent Spirits, Inc., Chicago

Pastoral Andersonville, Chicago

Perman Wine Selections, Chicago

Plum Market Old Town, Chicago

Red & White Wines, Chicago

Vin Chicago

LOUISIANA

Hopper's Carte des Vins, New Orleans

Martin Wine Cellar, New Orleans

MAINE

Maine & Loire Wine Shop, Portland

MARYLAND

Cordial Craft Wine, Beer & Spirits, Washington, DC

MacArthur Beverages, Washington, DC

MASSACHUSETTS

Lower Falls Wine Co., Newton

MONTANA

City Vineyard, Billings

Good Food Store, Missoula

Island Liquor Store, Helena

Missoula Wine Merchants, Missoula

The Gourmet Cellar, Livingston

Vino Per Tutti, Bozeman

NEW MEXICO

Jubilation Wine & Spirits, Albuquerque

Kokoman Fine Wines, Santa Fe

La Casa Sena, Santa Fe

Susan's Fine Wine & Spirits, Santa Fe

NEW YORK

Astor Wines & Spirits, New York City

Chambers Street Wines, New York City

Chelsea Wine Vault, New York City

Convive Wine & Spirits, New York City

Crush Wines & Spirits, New York City

Dandelion Wine, Brooklyn

Flatiron Wines & Spirits, New York City

Hudson Wine Merchants, Hudson

Leon & Son Wine and Spirits, Brooklyn

New York Vintners, New York City

Red Feet Wine Market & Spirit Provisions, Ithaca

Sea Grape Wine Shop, New York City

Sherry-Lehmann Wine and Spirits, New York City

Thirst Wine Merchants, Brooklyn

Union Square Wine & Spirits, New York City

Verve Wine, New York City

Vintry Fine Wines, New York City

NEVADA

Craft Wine and Beer, Reno

OREGON

Corvallis Brewing Supply, Portland

E & R Wine Shop, Portland

Liner & Elsen, Portland

Vinopolis Wine Shop, Portland

Zupan's Markets, Portland

RHODE ISLAND

Bottles Fine Wine, Providence

TEXAS

Houston Wine Merchant, Houston

Pogo's Wine & Spirits, Dallas

The Austin Wine Merchant, AustiVinology Bottle Shop & Wine Bar, Houston

VERMONT

Deadlus Wine, Burlington

Village Wine and Coffee, Shelburne

Windham Wines, Brattleboro

WASHINGTON

Bar Ferdinand, Seattle

Bin 41, Seattle

McCarthy & Schiering Wine Merchants, Seattle

Picnic, Seattle

Pike and Western Wine Shop, Seattle

Rain City Wines, Bothell

Rose's Café, Eastsound (Orcas Island)

RESOURCES

The Guild of Sommeliers
www.guildsomm.com

Kermit Lynch Wine Merchant
www.kermitlynch.com

Skurnik Wine & Spirits
www.skurnik.com

VOS Selections
www.vosselections.com

Published in 2017 by
Harper Design
An Imprint of HarperCollins Publishers
195 Broadway
New York, NY 10007
Tel: (212) 207-7000
Fax: (855) 746-6023
harperdesign@harpercollins.com
www.hc.com

Distributed throughout the world by
HarperCollins Publishers
195 Broadway
New York, NY 10007

ISBN 978-0-06-267620-7
Library of Congress Control Number 2016958627

Printed in the United States of America
First Printing, 2017

Cover and book design by
Shubhani Sarkar, sarkardesignstudio.com